Nong's
Thai Kitchen

84 CLASSIC RECIPES THAT ARE QUICK
HEALTHY AND DELICIOUS

NONGKRAN DAKS
and
ALEXANDRA GREELEY

TUTTLE Publishing

Tokyo | Rutland, Vermont | Singapore

Contents

My Love Affair with Thai Food

When I first arrived in Thailand as a young Peace Corps volunteer, Thai food was the last thing on my mind. It was 1975, and my knowledge of Thailand was minuscule. I knew a bit of history, a smattering of geography, and a teaspoonful of culture; but the wonderful, unique and irresistible pleasures of Thai food and cooking? I had no idea what good things were just around the corner for me. Falling in love with Thai food was easy, as it is for many people, whether they encounter it in Thailand or away from its gorgeous, generous, and abundant homeland.

My love and affection for the food of Thailand has continued to grow and deepen to this day. Decades after my time in Thailand, I remain fascinated by Thai cuisine, eager for any opportunity to eat it, read about it, and cook it at home. I also love to talk about it with people who share my passion, who love exploring and learning about the ingredients, traditions, recipes, and dishes that have made Thai food a source of pleasure and satisfaction around the world.

I returned home from Peace Corps determined to bring Thai food into my kitchen, despite the challenges of obtaining Thai ingredients here in North Carolina in the 1980s. Bicycling to the morning market where sheaves of lemongrass bordered mountains of chilies, fragrant herbs, crunchy vegetables, and fantastically sweet mangoes? A lovely memory, but not a feasible option for cooking Thai at home. A local Korean-owned Asian market, however, supplied me with the essentials: fish sauce, red and green curry paste, coconut milk, palm sugar, dried galangal, jasmine rice, and chilies galore. Along with limes, cucumbers, peanuts, shallots, garlic, eggplant, and cilantro from the supermarket, I was ready to get cooking—and that's what I did.

Within a few years, I was teaching Thai cooking classes and writing about Thai food for newspapers and magazines. Then came cookbooks, which led to my good fortune in meeting Nongkran Daks. I remember seeing her presentation on Thai cuisine at a conference for food professionals in Washington, DC, around ten years ago. I loved her energetic, generous, knowledgeable spirit and the way she brought the deeper story of Thai culture forward while offering tips on ingredients and apt points on technique. I bought her books and began to benefit from her knowledge personally, as she became my source on Thai language and classic and regional dishes which were unknown to me. Nong shared one of her recipes, a fantastic noodle dish from her Southern Thai tradition, allowing me to include it in one of my Thai cookbooks.

When I learned that Bobby Flay was heading to Nong's lovely DC-area restaurant, Thai Basil, for one of his signature Throwdowns, I smiled. He knows his stuff, but nobody throws down Pad Thai like Nongkran Daks! I wisely placed my bets on my friend, who of course won the day. Visiting her restaurant is a treat for anyone, but for people like me, who long for the food we remember enjoying in Thailand, it is a particular delight. From her exquisite Chicken Wrapped in Pandan Leaves and Shrimp Soup with Coconut Milk and Thai Ginger, to her sublime Watercress Salad with Shrimp, Spicy Beef with Mint Leaves, and Roasted Duck Curry with Wild Eggplants and Tomatoes, Nong's Thai menu transports her guests to Thailand for just a little while.

When Nong told me that she was working on this comprehensive book, I was thrilled and delighted for two reasons. One is that I love having Thai food known and shared, anywhere, anytime. I'm glad that Nong's deep, unique lifetime of knowledge and mastery of her cuisine will be made available to the world. I'm also selfishly glad for myself, because I am still learning about this extraordinary, sparklingly unique, complex way of cooking. I cannot imagine a better guide, instructor, inspiration, and mentor for any of us who love Thai food and long to understand it, learn about it, and become fluent in its pleasures and delights.

Nong's expertise stems from a lifetime spent in the Thai kitchen, literally beginning in her childhood and continuing to this day. She has cooked in Thailand, offered cooking classes, lectures and presentations, and headed up her own restaurant kitchens. She is also a mother who knows well the challenges of making meals for family at home. Given Nong's family's life, this has meant cooking around the world, including Bangkok, Taiwan, Pakse and Vientiane in Laos, Beijing, and her current home here in the US.

Whether you're just beginning the journey or you are, like me, a longtime devotee of Thailand's amazing cuisine, there's never been a better time to learn about Thai cooking. Thai ingredients are available on the shelves of many supermarkets, and the recent profusion of Asian markets, huge Asian grocery stores, and homegrown Asian ingredients in farmer's markets and CSA boxes makes it even easier.

I love Nongkran's food, I love her restaurant, and I love the way she writes recipes and shares her wisdom with everyone who wants to learn what makes Thai cooking special and how to bring it home. We are lucky that she and Alexandra Greeley have made the time to write this splendid, beautiful, practical and delightful cookbook, so that we can enjoy Nong's amazing Thai food at home.

At last, I can have Nong in the kitchen with me—and so can you.

Nancie McDermott
Author of *Southern Pies: A Gracious Plenty of Pie Recipes, from Lemon Chess to Chocolate Pecan,* and food blogger at
nanciemcdermott.com

Nongkran, Pad Thai Champion!

In the past several decades, many Americans have explored ethnic and often exotic cuisines, welcoming flavors and ingredients that rarely appear on the average American dinner table. Thai food, with its balanced flavors and textures, has staged a major American success. Thai-centric restaurants, Thai-inspired recipes, and Thai cookbooks have gained the public spotlight. You can walk down any street in almost any town in the USA and find a Thai restaurant dishing out pad Thai and chicken with basil. Not surprisingly, a number of Thai chefs have gained celebrity status. One who stands out is Nongkran Daks, owner of Thai Basil restaurant in Chantilly, Virginia and the winner of the Food Network's "Pad Thai Throwdown with Bobby Flay."

A native of Chumporn province in Southern Thailand, Nongkran Daks may well have been born to cook. She certainly began her kitchen life at an early age. Nongkran recalls that at age seven, when living with her sister-in-law in the small town of Langsuan, she was required to make ten curry pastes each afternoon to sell at the local open market. At her first lesson, she was seated before all the curry ingredients arranged in piles on trays and instructed to pound together the makings for each paste with a mortar and pestle.

Unlike other cooks, whose first kitchen foray might be boiling or frying eggs, hers was making authentic Thai curries from scratch. Gradually, cooking transformed itself from something she had to do to something she couldn't live without.

As she matured, Nongkran continued to cook, preparing and serving luncheon foods for her schoolmates at the request of her teachers. "My head teacher would ask me to make Panang curry and stewed pork with egg," she remembers. She cooked the dishes in the school kitchen and wrapped each serving in a banana leaf for separate lunch packets. The teachers chose Nongkran for this task because they knew she cooked well, and though it took time, they also knew she could keep up with her studies.

After high school, Nongkran moved to Bangkok, where she attended Chulalongkorn University's preparatory school. After graduation, she attended Kasetsart University, where she studied agricultural economics and lived in a dorm for the first few years. Her friends, knowing about her kitchen skills and her love of cooking, would ask her to cook for them. "Every Friday I rode my bike back home," she says. "My friends had collected money for me to buy ingredients so I could make them curries when I came back on Monday."

Upon graduation from Kasetsart in 1965, Nongkran married Larry Daks, an American Peace Corps volunteer who was teaching at that university; she was both his student and his Thai language teacher.

Over the years, the couple has lived in the US and in various locations throughout Asia, including China, Laos, Taiwan and Thailand. During one of their stays in Bangkok, Nongkran ran a snack bar called Nong's Kitchen, which featured Thai and Western food, including an outstanding cheesecake.

Thailand is also where Nongkran began to teach cooking. Most of her students were fellow Thais who wanted to learn more about their own cuisine and that of neighboring counties, but she soon began to expand her clientele.

During one stay in Beijing, Nongkran started catering parties for foreign diplomats, because few international foods or restaurants were available at the time. She often catered for the American embassy as well, especially after staff members had tasted and requested her special Chicken Satay with peanut satay sauce (page 34). She also conducted cooking classes in Beijing, where people were just starting to discover Thai food. "There was a lot of demand for Thai food," she remembers. "And also in Beijing, we were very close to Thailand and people from the embassy went there for R & R. People who had not known Thai food before fell in love with it." Expats in the American community in particular praised her cooking, and a number of them encouraged her to open a restaurant.

When Nongkran moved back to the Washington, DC area permanently in 1996, she continued to cook for friends

From Top to Bottom: Making Pad Thai (page 114) in Winnipeg. A close-up of the finished dish. Nong and television host Samantha Brown preparing to cook.

and local Asian festivals, and offered cooking classes in her home. She finally began to look into finding a real outlet—a restaurant—for her cooking passion. She got the opportunity when a Thai friend decided to sell her restaurant in Chantilly. Within days, Nongkran had opened up Thai Basil, which is now a major player in the Washington, DC restaurant world. She also became a member of Les Dames d'Escoffier, the prestigious women-only culinary group, and has been asked to give talks and to hold cooking classes and demonstrations throughout the mid-Atlantic region.

After her victory in the Throwdown and a subsequent appearance on the Travel Channel, Nongkran has become something of a local legend. Thai Basil and her regular cooking classes continue to draw patrons not only from the immediate area, but from both coasts and Canada, and even from Thailand itself. She is widely noted for using traditional Thai recipes without modifying them for Western tastes—she prefers to educate Western-ers' palates. For this reason, Nongkran is particularly proud that Thai Basil is one of the few restaurants in the United States to earn the Thai Select Award, a recognition of excellence awarded by the Thai Ministry of Commerce.

About Thai Food

Capturing the hearts, minds, and palates of a global audience, Thai food really is the stuff of gastronomic dreams: its flavors are a balance of sweet, salty, hot, and sour, and a recipe's components are thoughtfully composed to provide texture as well as balanced flavors. The ingredients may include just about anything that walks, crawls, or swims. In Chiang Mai, in the northern part of Thailand, for example, locals may enjoy grilled snakes or ants or crickets, or even fried bamboo worms. Elsewhere, water bugs and (reportedly) scorpions add a protein element to the diet. And on everyone's dining table, the produce—from the familiar long beans and the less-familiar marble-sized eggplants to the aromatic durian and crunchy water convolvulus—is supremely fresh. Street vendors, home cooks, and professionals in upscale kitchens alike can use traditional techniques and ingredients and individualize recipes to suit a mood or to appeal to modern tastes.

Tracing the development of Thai cooking reveals several influences. In studying the numerous cultural and culinary elements that have shaped Thai cooking, food historians have determined that migrant Chinese, Indians, Burmese, and Europeans passing through ancient Siam (now Thailand) left their imprint on the country's cuisine over the centuries. Neighboring Southeast Asian peoples from Vietnam, Laos, Cambodia, Malaysia, and Burma have influenced their Thai neighbors as well. In the north and northeast regions of Thailand, for example, dishes such as the Green Papaya Salad from Laos (page 66) and the hearty coconut-milk-based curry from Burma known as *Khao Soi* (page 108), have become culinary mainstays.

Chinese cooks also made three major contributions to Thai cuisine: rice, including the rice porridge known locally as *chok* (pronounced "joke"); noodles, a key ingredient in many dishes, particularly in the classic dish known as Pad Thai (page 114); and the versatile cooking vessel, the wok. Fish sauce, an essential component of Thai cuisine, also originated in China. Even Portuguese missionaries contributed an important element to Thai cooking: the chili, introduced from South America. The missionaries inspired Thai cooks to incorporate the fiery chili heat into many recipes. In fact, the legend surrounding the creation of one recipe, Crying Tiger (page 44), holds that the addition of chilies resulted in a dish so hot it made tigers cry.

Thai cooks rely on an array of basic seasonings to impart distinctively Thai flavors tho food. These include ingredients such as fish sauce, garlic, lemongrass, coconut milk, palm sugar, kaffir limes, galangal, fresh coriander and coriander seeds, shallots, and dried shrimp.

Regardless of nationality, anyone who embraces this Southeast Asian cuisine should understand how a traditional or typical meal is served. Thais prefer communal eating, and their main meals generally consist of multiple courses served family style. These may include a soup; a curry; a grilled, stir-fried, or steamed meat or seafood; assorted condiments; perhaps a salad served as an appetizer; and fruit or a simple sweet for dessert. It is common practice to scoop rice onto the plate and take a portion of one of the main dishes to eat alongside the rice before taking a serving of another dish. All courses are usually served at the same time, except for dessert.

Breakfasts and lunches are lighter, and may center on fried rice or noodles with a meat or vegetable garnish. As elsewhere in

Asia, rice—usually eaten morning, noon, and night—is basic to the cuisine. This staple is a bland counterpoint and welcome relief beside the rich, savory, and spicy stir-fries, curries, and grilled dishes. Thais often turn to rice porridge as a palate cleanser; or, if the meal has been minimal, a filling dish. When not at the table, Thais snack on the portable treats that are seemingly offered at every turn. Street and market vendors—their baskets, stands, and grills full of meats, noodles, soups, and sweets—are a common sight along city sidewalks and in open-air country markets. For a list of basic Thai ingredients, see page 14.

Contrary to what foreigners may assume, Thais generally use only a fork and a spoon, rather than chopsticks, at meals; the fork neatly pushes the food onto the spoon for easier eating. Except for some noodle dishes, Thai food is not usually eaten with chopsticks.

Aware of the growing global popularity of Thai food, the Thai government has been working diligently over the past decade to increase both the appreciation of Thai cooking and the establishment of Thai restaurants in such emerging markets as Dubai and Saudi Arabia, as well as Italy, Russia, and the Czech Republic. One of the first governmental pushes to promote Thai food occurred in 2002, when the Thai government sought to make Thai food more widely available across the globe. The campaign has been a resounding success, with the number of Thai restaurants worldwide rising from 5,500 to 20,000 as of 2013, according to a spokesman for the Thai National Innovation Agency.

According to a 2011 estimate from the Thai government's Foreign Office, 5,000 of these restaurants are located in the US. In addition, many American restaurant kitchens now borrow extensively from the

Thai spice shelf, just to give their menus an exotic spin. Furthermore, most supermarkets have begun stocking Thai-centric ingredients such as curry pastes or stalks of fresh lemongrass. Even some mass-marketing of Thai flavors has occurred, like the (ultimately unsuccessful) attempt by Subway to sell a Thai chicken sandwich in mid-2000. The California Pizza Kitchen is one of the national franchises that have taken Thai food seriously: it features a Thai-style pizza.

In response to the burgeoning popularity of Thai food in the United States, the Royal Thai Counsel in Los Angeles has appointed the first Culinary Ambassador of Thai Cuisine, a young Thai chef named Jet Tila. His duties include touring the country to showcase Thai cooking in all its authentic glory. Indeed, the National Innovation Agency is trying to standardize popular Thai dishes such as Pad Thai (page 114) and *Tom Yum*

From Left to Right: Nong teaching at CulinAerie Cooking School in Washington, DC.; Steamed seafood in banana-leaf cups; Rice Soup with Shrimp (page 54); Nong in the kitchen of Thai Basil in Chantilly, VA.

(page 50) in order to offer authentic Thai recipes. The agency has realized that many cooks in Thai restaurants are not natives of Thailand.

The intense focus on Thai cooking and Thai restaurants is good news for the well-traveled American public seeking authentic Thai meals. It has helped to set the stage for chefs like Nongkran Daks to showcase their skills. For this reason, the compendium of traditional Thai recipes perfected by Nongkran Daks which you now hold in your hands is a real treasure. Welcome to *Nong's Thai Kitchen.*

Nongkran Daks
นงคราม แดกส์

Thai Ingredients and Utensils

Though Thai cuisine varies widely, many recipes have common elements. The items described here can all be found at Asian markets or ordered on the Internet.

Bean curd: A staple of the Asian and Western vegetarian diet and a delicious protein substitute in any cuisine, bean curd (also called tofu) is made in a process similar to making cheese. Fresh bean curd, cut in large pieces or cubed, may be steamed, deep-fried, and stir-fried. Thais add bean curd to many dishes, including soups, stews, and curries. If refrigerated and placed in water, fresh bean curd keeps well for a few days.

Cardamom: A member of the same family as ginger, cardamom produces tiny seeds in a straw-colored pod that add an elusive flavor and fragrance to many Thai dishes, particularly curries. Thai cardamom is milder than the Indian version. Cardamom is readily available at Asian and Western markets.

Chinese broccoli: This Asian relative of Western broccoli has long, slender stems and tops with narrow leaves. Pop-

Chilies: Many different sizes, shapes, and colors of chili are used in Thai cooking, all of which add a level of heat and flavor so typical of this Asian cuisine. The most commonly used chilies are the small, pointed red, green, or red-orange bird's eye chilies, which produce a fiery taste, and the much milder finger-length chilies. Dried chilies require a brief soaking before being ground into a curry paste. Thai chilies are readily available at Asian markets and at some well-stocked Western supermarkets. The general Thai word for chilies is *prik*.

Bird's Eye Chilies

Green and Red Finger Chilies

Dried Chilies

Coconut cream/coconut milk: Although the names may seem interchangeable, coconut cream and coconut milk are really two different ingredients. Traditionally, Thais grate fresh coconuts and soak the shreds in hot water; the first pressing of the shreds yields coconut cream. A second soaking and pressing of shreds produces the thinner coconut milk. Coconut cream is suitable for frying, and is also the basis for several curries; the thinner milk is also a base for many curries. Only a few brands of Thai coconut cream are readily available in Asian markets.

These include Mae Ploy (the label says milk, but it contains only thick cream), Aroy-D, and Chaokoh. Coconut milk is much more readily available in Asian and Western markets than coconut cream. If it has not been shaken, a can of coconut milk may have an upper layer of thick cream and a layer of the thinner milk below. Some brands, however, contain none of the thick cream layer at all. It should be noted that one 13.5-ounce (400-ml) can contains about 2 cups of milk. Leftovers may be stored in a tightly sealed container for up to two days in the refrigerator or one month in the freezer.

---

ular in Cantonese cooking, this easy-to-prepare vegetable is available at most well-stocked supermarkets and at Asian markets. Its Cantonese name is *gai lan*. In Thailand, it is called *pak khana*.

Coriander: In all its forms, fresh coriander—also known as cilantro and Chinese parsley—is a staple of Thai cooking. The fragrant fresh leaves are often used as a garnish, while the roots, pounded together with garlic and black pepper, provide a basic seasoning for many dishes. Dried and toasted coriander seeds form the basis of many different curry pastes, as well as the seasoning for Thai Beef Jerky (page 30). Fresh coriander is readily available year round at Asian and Western markets. If you wish to make Thai Pesto Paste (page 24), look for bunches with the roots still attached; these will require very thorough rinsing to wash away the grit.

Fish sauce: Also known as *nam pla*, fish sauce is a staple of Thai cooking. This distinctive sauce is made from salted, fermented fish or small shrimp. Fish sauce is widely available, but quality and taste vary; generally speaking, the quality of the sauce increases with the price. It keeps for several years stored in a cool, dry place.

Galangal: This rhizome, also known as Thai ginger or *kha*, is a close relative of ginger, which it resembles in appearance but not in flavor. Fresh galangal, with its citrus-ginger taste, adds a unique essence to many Thai dishes, including stir-fries, soups, and curry pastes. If fresh galangal is not available, you may find dried sliced galangal, which you can rehydrate in boiling water; frozen galangal root; or powdered galangal. Fresh galangal will keep in the freezer for several months if tightly wrapped.

Kaffir lime: The small, knobby, fragrant lime known as *makrut* in Thailand is a key seasoning for many dishes. Although the lime itself has little juice, its grated rind and its leaves, either whole or shredded, add a distinctive flavor to soups, curries, and stir-fries. Rarely found fresh even at Asian markets, pack-

aged kaffir limes are often sold frozen. Several online markets sell fresh kaffir lime leaves and whole limes. The shiny green leaves are so prized for their unique flavor that Thais often grow their own kaffir lime trees for easy access. Though more readily available, Western limes and their leaves and rinds are not a suitable substitute.

Lemongrass: An essential component of many Thai dishes, the highly aromatic lemongrass stalks impart a lemony fragrance and flavor. The plump root end of the tough stalks must be peeled and then pounded or ground up when used in a curry or for a soup seasoning to release the flavor. While only the fleshy, yellowish part of the stalk is digestible, Thai cooks often use the full stalk in a soup or curry and remove it before serving. One stalk yields several tablespoons of sliced or chopped lemongrass. All Asian and many Western markets carry fresh lemongrass, but in a pinch, dried and powdered lemongrass can be used. Fresh lemongrass freezes well for several months. There are no equivalents.

Mortar and pestle: Before the age of food processors, the traditional large stone mortar and pestle were necessary pieces of kitchen equipment in Thailand, for it was with these that Thai cooks pounded ingredients together to make the basic paste for curry seasonings. According to an old wives' tale, a young suitor would walk through a Thai village listening to the noise of pounding. If the action sounded sure and swift, he would go in and ask for the young girl's hand in marriage, as this meant she would be a good home cook.

Oyster sauce: Made from oyster extract, soy sauce, and water, oyster sauce is readily available in Asian and Western markets. It is a much-used seasoning in many dishes, and goes well with noodles, seafood, vegetables, bean curd, and meat.

Types of Fresh Rice Noodles

Dried Egg Noodles   Mung Bean Noodles

Fresh Egg Noodles   Dried Vermicelli

Noodles: Although Thai cooks incorporate a variety of noodles in their meals, those most commonly used include thick, flat fresh rice noodles; dried rice noodles; slender dried vermicelli; brittle mung bean noodles; and fresh or dried egg noodles. Dried noodles used as accompaniments to curries usually require cooking and draining ahead of time; otherwise, they may be added directly to a soup. Fresh rice noodles that are coated with oil need no further preparation; if you rinse them, they may fall apart during cooking.

Palm sugar: Made from the sap of the coconut palm or the sugar palm tree, palm sugar is a popular Asian sweetener. The caramel-colored Thai palm sugar comes in the form of solid blocks or discs of varying sizes; it is also available as a semi-soft sugar in a jar. While less sweet than granulated sugar, it still imparts a sweet undertone wherever it is used. Thai palm sugar is available in most Asian markets and from online Asian grocers. If palm sugar is not available, substitute soft brown sugar or granulated sugar with a bit of maple syrup instead.

Pomelo: This large citrus fruit, native to Southeast Asia, resembles a thick-skinned grapefruit. It weighs between two and four pounds and has a sweet or mildly tart flavor. The thick pale-yellow skin is easy to peel, but because the membrane covering each segment may be bitter and tough, segments are usually peeled before eating. Thais eat pomelos as a dessert as well as in salads.

Shrimp, dried and paste:
Tiny air- or sun-dried shrimp

add a slightly fishy and salty flavor to many dishes. They are available in most Asian markets, as well as some supermarkets. Be sure that the shrimp are still somewhat pinkish, hence fresh, and have not turned gray or white with age. If a recipe calls for shrimp powder, dry roast some dried shrimp, then pulverize in a blender or food processor. Shrimp paste ranges in color from pink to dark brown, with the pink used in curries and the darker paste used in dipping sauces. Shrimp paste should always be cooked before using, even if the recipe does not call for cooking. To use shrimp paste, wrap it in banana leaves and

grill it before adding it to other ingredients.

Strainer: Wire-mesh strainers like the one shown here are commonplace in Asia. They are useful for skimming and scooping out items such as dumplings, noodles, and egg rolls from liquids or when deep-fat frying. The handles are usually made of bamboo.

Rice: A staple of the Thai diet, cooked rice is served at almost every meal to accompany curries. Steamed rice is served with grilled foods in the northeast part of Thailand; rice is also made into the Thai porridge known as *chok* and incorporated into desserts. The fragrant long-grain variety may be the best-known Thai rice,

although new, organic strains of rice are now finding their way to the market. Counted among the most popular strains, it remains costlier than other kinds of rice, as it expands relatively little when it is cooked. Thais use many other rice varieties, including a long-grain glutinous type called sticky rice that is used in desserts and, particularly

in northern and northeast Thailand, served with savory dishes. Regardless of type, rice is easily and quickly prepared either in a rice cooker or simply in a cookpot on the stove. Sticky rice must be soaked first, then steamed rather than boiled (see page 27). Black sticky rice is also used as a starch in some Thai desserts (see page 145).

Thai Jasmine Rice

Black Sticky Rice

Sticky Rice

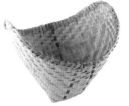

Bamboo Baskets   **Woven Bamboo Basket**

Steamers: Thais use several kinds of steamers for their cooking. The woven bamboo baskets used for steaming sticky rice fit into a large metal steamer pot that holds boiling water. Round woven-bamboo steamers have one or two tiers for stacking when cooking dumplings or Thai sweets; these rest on a metal rack inside a cookpot of boiling water. Also essential are tiered metal steamers of varying sizes. These generally consist of two layers, with the bottom one holding boiling water. They are useful for steaming seafood, dumplings, vegetables, or even sticky rice. (For sticky rice, line the upper layer with cheesecloth and place the rice on top.)

Tamarind: The bushy tamarind tree produces an edible pod-like fruit. When the dried pod is soaked and then squeezed to remove the liquid, the interior flesh produces a slightly sour juice used to flavor many Thai dishes. Dried tamarind must be soaked for at least 10 minutes, then squeezed and strained through a sieve to remove seeds and fibrous material. Alternatively, tamarind paste is available in cans; this can be stored in the refrigerator indefinitely.

Thai basil: With its pointed dark green leaves, an edible purple flower and a slight minty taste, Thai basil, known in Thailand as *bai horapa*, is a tropical version of the more common Italian or Mediterranean basil, but the two basils are not interchangeable. Thai basil is readily available in Asian markets and in many supermarkets year round. My restaurant, Thai Basil, takes its name and symbol from this herb.

Thai eggplants: Several different varieties of eggplant are used in Thai cooking. These include the rather bitter pea-sized eggplants known as Thai wild eggplant or pea eggplant; the round green or white Thai eggplants, which are slightly larger than a golf ball; and the slender 8- to 10-inch-long purple, green, or white eggplants variously known as oriental, Asian, Japanese, or Chinese eggplants. Asian eggplants and round Thai eggplants are readily available in Asian markets, but the tiny Thai wild eggplant may be more difficult to find.

Basic Methods and Techniques

While items like pandan juice and tamarind juice may be available commercially, using fresh homemade versions makes for a huge difference in flavor.

Pandan Juice

Nam Bai Toey

The juice of pandan (also known as pandanus) leaves is the "vanilla" of Thai cuisine. This ingredient is used in desserts, and, on occasion, with rice and in drinks. It has a wonderfully distinctive flavor and a fragrance so pleasing that some taxi drivers keep it in the back of their cabs. You may also encounter the scent of pandan in the bathrooms of some Thai establishments and in flower arrangements. Commercially available pandan juice may also be used, but it doesn't compare with the flavor and aroma that the freshly made juice adds to dishes. Look for the leaves fresh or frozen in Asian supermarkets or dried from online markets. You can also purchase pandan leaf extract from Asian markets and on the internet.

Preparation time: 5 MINUTES
Makes 1/2 CUP (125 ML)

1 cup (130 g) chopped pandan leaves
1/2 cup (125 ml) water

Combine pandan leaves and water in a blender and process until smooth. Drain through a sieve or squeeze through a cheesecloth into a container. Discard the leaves. Any leftover liquid should be frozen.

Tamarind Juice

Nam Makham

Tamarind paste is available in 8-oz (225-g) and 1-lb (450-g) packages in most Asian markets. This juice can be refrigerated for up to a week; after that, it may turn rancid.

Preparation time: 1 MINUTE, PLUS 20 MINUTES FOR SOAKING
Makes 1 CUP (250 ML)

Break off $1/3$ cup (100 g) tamarind paste and place in a nonreactive bowl. Add 1 cup (250 ml) warm water. Let the tamarind soak for 30 minutes, then squeeze and knead the paste until it dissolves. Strain out seeds and fiber, and either use or store the resulting liquid.

Pandan Juice

How to Make Toasted Rice

1 For best flavor, rice should be freshly toasted. If you only cook Thai food occasionally, just make a little at a time so the toasted rice doesn't lose its fragrance. As I cook Thai food frequently, I make a cup at a time and keep the unused portion in a tightly closed jar in the refrigerator.
2 Dry-fry uncooked white sticky rice in a wok or skillet over low heat, stirring frequently. To enhance the fragrance, add 4 to 5 slices of galangal or lemongrass. Keep frying until the grains are deep golden-brown, about 13 minutes.
3 Let toasted rice cool, and then grind in a spice grinder until it resembles corn-meal.

How to Roll-Cut Vegetables

Long, cylindrical vegetables like carrots, zucchini, daikon radish, Asian eggplants, or Chinese okra are best suited for roll-cutting. I particularly recommend this technique if the vegetables are to be pickled or stir-fried. Asian cooks often roll-cut vegetables in order to expose more surface area to the heat. Roll-cut shapes are also attractive, making for a nice presentation.

1 Wash and peel the vegetable.
2 Lay the vegetable on a cutting board. Position your knife at a 45-degree angle, maintaining a firm grip on the vegetable. With a diagonal cut, remove the thick end and discard. Then roll the vegetable a quarter turn toward you and make another diagonal cut. Repeat until you reach the end. Discard the last piece.
3 This process produces multi-faceted pieces that gain maximum flavor when stir-fried or pickled.

How to Toast Seeds

Spread the seeds in a layer on a clean baking sheet and toast them in a 350°F (175°C) oven, stirring frequently, for 5 minutes or until fragrant and lightly browned. It may be easier to toast the amount needed in a dry skillet over low heat, stirring frequently, until the seeds are toasted. This may take just a few minutes depending on the type of seed and its size. You can also microwave seeds on high heat for 2 minutes, stirring after 1 minute to be sure they toast evenly.

How to Toast Coconut

1 Coconut is toasted much as seeds are. Spread coconut flakes in a shallow baking pan. Toast in a 350°F (175°C) oven for 15 to 20 minutes or until lightly browned.
2 If you only need a small amount, you can toast coconut in a frying pan over low heat, stirring frequently until lightly browned, about 7 to 10 minutes. You can also microwave on high for 3 minutes, stirring every minute.

Basic Recipes

These recipes and techniques are fundamental to many of the dishes included in this book. Some of the seasonings are available commercially, but they are far superior when made fresh.

Thai Chili Paste
Nam Prik Pao

This versatile Thai sauce really does wonders for a variety of foods. It goes well with Spicy Lemongrass Soup (*Tom Yum*); in noodle dishes like *Ba Mee Nam Prik Pao*; and with fried rice (see page 111). When my refrigerator and pantry are almost bare, or I just don't know what to eat, I mix this magic sauce with hot jasmine rice, accompanied by a hard-boiled egg, and I feel like I'm in heaven! You can purchase ready-made Thai chili paste, but making it yourself results in a much better product. The sauce should taste sweet, sour, and salty. This chili paste will keep for months in the refrigerator in a tightly sealed container.

Preparation time: 10 MINUTES
Cooking time: 8 MINUTES
Makes ABOUT 1 CUP (225 G)

1 cup (250 ml) vegetable oil for deep-frying
15 shallots, peeled and sliced
10 garlic cloves, peeled and sliced
¼ cup (120 g) dried shrimp
7 dried finger or Thai chilies, seeded
Five ⅛-in (3 mm) thick slices galangal
5 tablespoons palm sugar
3 tablespoons thick Tamarind Juice (page 20)
1 tablespoon fish sauce
1 teaspoon salt

1 Heat the oil in a large wok over medium-high heat. Deep-fry the shallots, garlic cloves, dried shrimp, chilies, and galangal one by one.
2 Place the deep-fried ingredients in a blender. Some of the oil used for frying may be added to facilitate the blending. Once it is puréed, place the mixture in a saucepan and bring to a boil. Add the palm sugar, tamarind juice, fish sauce, and salt, and reduce the heat to low. Cook, stirring regularly until the mixture thickens, about 5 minutes. The mixture will have a jamlike consistency; in fact, some people call this sauce "chili jam."

Red Curry Paste *Nam Prik Kang Dang*

It used to be hard to find many of the basic ingredients for making either the red or green curry paste except at Asian markets. Because of the increasing interest in Thai and other Asian cuisines, however, they are now available at many well-stocked supermarkets and from online Asian grocers. Making these pastes from scratch is worth the extra effort. Unlike the canned versions, homemade pastes are vibrant and aromatic. Besides, these pastes add a flavor element to other Thai dishes, including stir-fries and fried rice.

Preparation time: 5 MINUTES, PLUS 20 MINUTES FOR SOAKING
Makes 1 CUP (225 G)

10 whole black peppercorns
5 dried red chilies
Three 1/2-in (3-mm) thick slices galangal, shredded
3 shallots, peeled and coarsely chopped
3 cloves garlic
2 fresh coriander roots
1/4 cup (60 g) thinly sliced lemongrass
1 teaspoon toasted coriander seeds
1 teaspoon kaffir lime zest
1 teaspoon shrimp paste
1/2 teaspoon ground cumin
1 teaspoon salt
1/2 cup (125 ml) water

1 Soak the dried chilies in cold water for 20 minutes, then squeeze dry.
2 Combine all ingredients in a blender and blend on high until smooth.
3 Paste may be refrigerated in a tightly sealed container for 1 week or frozen for up to 3 months.

Note: Vegetarians can substitute 1 tablespoon bean paste (*tao jiao*) for the 1 teaspoon shrimp paste.
   Red curry paste is particularly versatile, and makes a delicious addition to dry curries, fish cakes, fried rice, and Steamed Seafood Curry (page 96). It adds flavor to the peanut sauce for Chicken Satay (page 34)— though be careful to reduce the number of chilies for making the sauce. This recipe is for a basic red curry paste. Unused portions may be stored for up to two weeks in the refrigerator in a tightly sealed container.

Green Curry Paste

Nam Prik Kang Kheaw

Green curry paste can be as spicy as red, but the coriander leaves lend it a subtly herbal flavor.

Preparation time: 5 MINUTES
Makes 1 CUP (225 G)

5 fresh dark green Thai finger chilies or
    jalapeños
3 shallots, peeled and quartered
3 cloves garlic, peeled
Three 1/8-in (3-mm) thick slices galangal,
    shredded
1/4 cup (50 g) thinly sliced lemongrass
2 fresh coriander roots, coarsely chopped
1 stem fresh coriander with leaves, coarsely
    chopped
2 teaspoons coriander seeds, toasted
1 teaspoon cumin seeds, toasted
1 teaspoon coarsely chopped kaffir lime zest
1 teaspoon salt
1 teaspoon shrimp paste
10 whole black peppercorns
1/2 cup (125 ml) water

Combine all ingredients in a blender and blend on high until smooth. Store any unused paste in a sealed container in the fridge for 1 week, or keep frozen for up to 3 months.

Thai Pesto Paste

Fresh coriander stems may be used if the roots are not available, although the flavor will not be exactly the same. This paste freezes well, so when you find fresh coriander with roots, make Thai Pesto and freeze it until needed. When a recipe calls for it, you can scoop out the amount you need and leave the remainder in the freezer for future use.

Preparation time: 4 MINUTES
Makes 2 HEAPING TABLESPOONS

4 garlic cloves, peeled
3 fresh coriander roots, including
    3-in (7.5-cm) stems, coarsely
    chopped
1/2 teaspoon black peppercorns
1/2 teaspoon salt

Be sure the coriander roots are well washed and free of grit. Pound all ingredients with a mortar and pestle until they form a paste. Alternatively, process in a blender with enough water to form a paste.

Sweet and Hot Sauce

Nam Jim

Actually, in Thailand we don't refrigerate this sauce, since the vinegar acts as a preservative and it's used within a few days. However, it can be stored in the refrigerator in a tightly lidded container for several months. I've never tried to freeze it. This dip is great with stuffed chicken wings, barbecued chicken, and other Thai dishes that call for a sweet and hot sauce. Look for the fresh chili paste, also called *sambal oelek*, and Thai plum sauce, or *nam buoi*, in Asian markets or from online Asian grocers.

Preparation time: 2 MINUTES
Cooking time: 40 MINUTES
Makes 2 CUPS (500 ML)

1 cup (200 g) granulated sugar
1/2 cup (125 ml) water
1/2 cup (125 ml) vinegar
1/4 cup (60 ml) Thai plum sauce
1 teaspoon ground fresh chili paste
3 garlic cloves, finely chopped

Combine the sugar, water, and vinegar in a small saucepan. Bring the mixture to a boil over high heat. Reduce the heat to low, and cook until the mixture starts to thicken, about 40 minutes. Add the plum sauce, chili paste, and garlic. Stir a few times, and remove from the heat to cool.

Sriracha Chili Sauce

Nam Prik Sriracha

Thais serve this delicious sauce with many dishes, such as omelets and Crispy Mussel Pancakes (page 71). It is also good with grilled and deep-fried dishes. The commercial Sriracha sauce produced in Thailand, which differs from the version produced in California, is available in three levels of spiciness: mild, medium, and hot. The name of the sauce comes from the seaside village southeast of Bangkok where it is manufactured. This is my homemade version of this versatile condiment.

Preparation time: 5 MINUTES
Cooking time: 10 MINUTES
Makes 1 1/2 CUPS (375 ML)

1 cup (250 ml) water
1 tablespoon Thai fish sauce
1 tablespoon sugar
9 fresh red finger chilies, coarsely chopped
4 cloves garlic, coarsely chopped
1/2 teaspoon sea salt or kosher salt
1/4 cup (60 ml) distilled white vinegar

1 Combine the water, fish sauce, sugar, chilies, garlic and salt in a small saucepan and bring to a boil over medium-high heat. Reduce the heat to low and cook the mixture until the garlic and chilies are tender, about 5 minutes. Remove from the heat and cool to room temperature.
2 Transfer the cooked ingredients to a blender. Add the vinegar and purée the mixture until smooth, about 1 minute. Stored in a tightly sealed container in the refrigerator, this sauce should last indefinitely.

Crispy Shallots or Garlic

Hom Lek/Kratiam Jiao

Thai-style fried shallots or fried garlic, imported from Thailand or Vietnam, are now available in Asian grocery stores. You can use the ready-made product, but the homemade version adds more flavor to your dishes. The shallots or garlic can be prepared in a microwave or fried in oil and drained on paper towels. Since microwaves vary in wattage, and shallots and garlic burn easily, monitor your cooking time carefully. Even after they are removed from the microwave, they will continue to cook.

Preparation time: 2 TO 3 MINUTES
Cooking time: 2 TO 3 MINUTES
Makes ABOUT 1/2 CUP (125 ML)

1/2 cup (100 g) peeled and thinly sliced shallots or garlic cloves
Vegetable oil to cover

1 Place sliced shallots or garlic cloves in a microwave-safe dish, such as a ramekin. Add oil to barely cover. Microwave on high for 1 minute and stir. Microwave for 1 minute more and stir again. When the shallots or garlic turn light brown, they're done.

2 Remove shallots or garlic from oil. Save the oil for stir-frying.

3 Alternatively, heat a tablespoon of oil in a wok or skillet and stir-fry the shallots or garlic, stirring constantly, until they turn light brown. Remove from the oil and allow to cool. Stored in an airtight container in your pantry, fried shallots or garlic will stay crisp for several days.

Steamed Jasmine Rice

This is a very old-fashioned way of cooking long-grain rice, but it works every time.

Preparation time: 2 MINUTES
Cooking time: 25 MINUTES
Makes 6 CUPS (1.2 KG) COOKED RICE

3 cups (600 g) jasmine rice
Water to cover the rice

1 Rinse the rice until the water runs clear. Drain and place in a saucepan or electric rice cooker. Add just enough water to cover about 1 inch above the rice. Another way of measuring the amount of water is to touch the surface of the rice in the pot with the index finger, then add just enough water to reach the first knuckle.
2 Bring the rice and water to a boil over medium heat. Reduce the heat to medium-low and cook uncovered for about 15 minutes. When almost all the liquid has been absorbed, reduce the heat to low, cover, and cook for 10 minutes more. Remove from heat and stir with a wooden spoon or with chopsticks before serving.
3 If you use an electric rice cooker, follow the manufacturer's instructions; the rice will cook automatically after you press the ON button.

Steamed Sticky Rice
Khao Niue Nung

Sticky rice—also called pearl rice, glutinous rice, or sweet rice—is the main carbohydrate in the northern and northeastern part of Thailand, where it is grown. Because it has more starch than other rice varieties, it is more filling, which is important in these traditionally poor regions. Due to the migration of people from northeastern Thailand, sticky rice and the dishes that accompany it have now become popular throughout the country.

Preparation time: 5 MINUTES, PLUS 6 HOURS FOR SOAKING
Cooking time: 25 MINUTES
Makes ABOUT 6 CUPS (1.2 KG) COOKED RICE

3 cups (700 g) sticky rice
8 cups (2 liters) cold water

1 Place the sticky rice in a bowl. Add enough cold water to cover the rice. Let the rice soak for at least 6 hours, or overnight.
2 Heat water in a steamer pot. When the water starts to boil, drain the rice and pour it into the woven basket top of a Thai steamer or another steamer that sits above the water. Cover the basket or pot and steam over high heat for 20 minutes. Stir the rice with a wooden spoon, then continue to steam for 5 minutes more.
3 Remove rice from heat and place in a separate container. Cover until ready to use.

Note: This rice has long been a popular ingredient in Thai snacks or desserts. Sticky rice is literally finger food: diners grab a handful of rice, roll it into a ball, and then dip the rice in a hot sauce or eat it with dishes such as Grilled Chicken (page 72), Green Papaya Salad (page 66), Spicy Beef with Mint Leaves (page 83), or Thai Beef Jerky (page 30).

Chapter 1

Thai Appetizers and Finger Food

In the past, Thais served finger foods or appetizers to accompany shots of whiskey or bottles of beer. Today, though almost every urban Thai enjoys finger foods and appetizers, these tasty snacks are not just relegated to cocktail parties. Instead, whether at home with guests or eating out at a restaurant, Thais will incorporate these small treats into the meal itself. "We would serve spicy, flavored foods, like *laap* or *yam nua*," says Nongkran Daks. "The dish 'Crying Tiger' (Grilled Beef with Roasted Rice Powder Dipping Sauce, page 44), which has grilled meat sliced up and served with a dipping sauce, is very popular." As for the Peanut Wafers (page 45), when Nongkran was a university student, she used to make them and sell them to earn money.

Thai Beef Jerky *Nua Sawan*

Nua Sawan in Thai literally means "heavenly beef." This dish is a slightly spicy style of beef jerky with a sweet undertone. Traditionally, Thais would dry the beef slices by laying them out in the hot sun for several hours. Today most people use the oven; you may also grill the meat over charcoal or gas outside. It is very convenient to use meat that has been precut for fajitas, which is sold in many supermarkets. This dish is often served with sticky rice, and goes great as snack food alongside a German-style Thai beer such as Chang or Singha, both of which can now be found outside of Thailand. Be sure to make more than one recipe—it will disappear fast!

Preparation time: 5 MINUTES, PLUS 2 HOURS FOR MARINATING
Cooking time: 35 MINUTES
Makes 4 TO 6 SERVINGS

3 tablespoons palm sugar
1 tablespoon fish sauce
1 tablespoon soy sauce
1 tablespoon coarsely ground coriander seeds
1/2 teaspoon salt
1 lb (500 g) beef, any cut, sliced about
   1/8 in (3 mm) thick
2 cups (500 ml) vegetable oil for frying

1 Combine the first 5 ingredients in a large nonreactive bowl. Marinate the beef for at least 2 hours or overnight in the refrigerator.
2 Preheat oven to 200°F (95°C). Arrange the meat on a baking rack in one layer. Bake until dried out, about 30 minutes.
3 Heat the oil to 350°F (175°C) and cook the meat until the pieces turn light brown, about 3 minutes. Remove from the oil and drain on paper towels.

Galloping Horses *Maa Hor*

This popular snack is an old-fashioned dish that Thais love. Its unusual name comes from the ancient Chinese, who in olden times would demand that their food be brought out quickly, as fast as a galloping horse—or in Mandarin, *ma hsang lai*. For the best results, use any fruit that has a slightly sour taste, preferably pineapple or oranges.

Preparation time: 20 MINUTES
Cooking time: 10 MINUTES
Makes 40 PIECES

Pork Mixture
3 garlic cloves, peeled
2 fresh coriander roots
1 tablespoon vegetable oil
1/2 lb (225 g) lean ground pork
4 tablespoons crushed roasted peanuts

Seasoning Sauce
2 tablespoons fish sauce
2 tablespoons palm sugar
1/2 teaspoon salt
1/8 teaspoon freshly ground black pepper

Forty 1-in x 2-in (2.5-cm x 5-cm) squares cut fresh fruit (pineapple or oranges are best)

Leaves from 2 sprigs fresh coriander
2 fresh Thai red finger chilies, sliced crosswise into rings

1 Pound the garlic and fresh coriander roots with a mortar and pestle until fine; alternately, process in a food processor.

2 In a nonstick skillet, stir-fry the pork over medium heat until it is cooked through, about 5 minutes.

3 As the pork is cooking, combine the seasoning sauce ingredients in a bowl and stir to mix well. Add the sauce to the pork, along with the peanuts, and continue to cook, stirring well, until all ingredients are combined and any liquid has evaporated. Remove from the heat and allow to cool.

4 To serve, take a piece of fruit and spoon 1 teaspoon of the pork mixture on it. Place the fruit on a serving dish; repeat. Garnish with coriander leaves and chili rings.

Siamese Chicken Wings Stuffed with Crab Meat _Peek Kai Yat Sai_

This appetizer is very popular at my restaurant, Thai Basil. It is time-consuming to make, but you can prepare the wings in advance and freeze them until ready to use. Just thaw them and deep-fry before serving. The wings can also be frozen after they are stuffed and baked. This homemade batter is light and makes the wings crispy. You can also use a commercial tempura batter, if you prefer. Just follow the package directions. If you are having a large gathering, you may want to double the recipe, because people love this dish. Battered and deep-fried vegetables such as cut-up eggplant, string beans, onions, green onions (scallions), sweet potatoes, pumpkin, and fresh asparagus are also delicious accompanied by Sweet and Hot Sauce. The Thai plum sauce, or _nam buoi_, and the fresh chili paste known as _sambal oelek_ called for in the sauce may be found in Asian markets or online. The recipe on page 22 makes about 1 cup of sauce. Store leftovers in the refrigerator.

Preparation time: 30 MINUTES, PLUS 30
MINUTES FOR SOAKING
Cooking time: 30 MINUTES
Makes 24 PIECES

Batter

1 cup (125 g) all-purpose flour
1 tablespoon cornstarch
$1/2$ teaspoon salt
$1/2$ teaspoon baking powder
1 cup (250 ml) very cold water

Stuffing

4 dried shiitake mushrooms, soaked in cold
water for 30 minutes
1 cup (130 g) uncooked bean thread
noodles, soaked in warm water for 30
minutes
1 cup (100 g) ground pork or chicken
1 cup (100 g) crabmeat, picked clean,
or minced peeled shrimp
$1/4$ cup (50 g) chopped water chestnuts
1 yellow onion, peeled and chopped
1 green onion (scallion), chopped
1 stem fresh coriander, chopped
1 small carrot, grated
3 garlic cloves, peeled and finely chopped
2 teaspoons salt
$1/2$ teaspoon granulated sugar
$1/2$ teaspoon ground white or black pepper

Chicken wings

24 chicken drumettes (the upper part of
the wing)
3 cups (750 ml) vegetable oil for deep-
frying
Sweet and Hot Sauce (page 25), for serving

1 Combine dry batter ingredients. Add the cold water and mix until batter is smooth. Set aside.

2 Rinse the soaked mushrooms and shred into small pieces. Cut the bean thread noodles into 1-inch (2.5-cm) long sections. Combine the remaining stuffing ingredients and mix well. Fold in the mushrooms and noodles. Set aside. Preheat oven to 350°F (175°C).

3 To prepare the chicken wings, separate the skin and tendons attached to the narrow end of the drumettes and push the meat gently down toward the thick end, keeping the skin intact. Gently push the meat-and-crab mixture into the pocket to fill. Repeat procedure for the remaining drumettes. Lay the drumettes flat in a baking pan.

4 Bake for 10 to 15 minutes. Remove from oven and allow to cool.

5 Meanwhile, heat the oil in a wok over medium heat to 375°F (190°C). When wings are cool, dip each one in batter. Deep-fry 4 or 5 pieces at a time until golden brown, 5 to 6 minutes. Drain on a paper towel and serve hot with Sweet and Hot Sauce.

Chicken Satay   *Sate Gai*

It has become easier to find authentic Thai dishes outside of Thailand. This is particularly true in cities such as Los Angeles, New York City, Chicago, and Washington, DC, where many native Thais live. Nevertheless, some easy-to-prepare dishes inevitably undergo changes. For example, this satay dish: In Thailand, satay is generally made with beef or pork, but in the United States you generally only find chicken satay.

This is true even in my Virginia restaurant, Thai Basil. When I first opened in 1999, I offered pork, beef, and chicken satay, but nobody ordered the pork or beef, so now we serve only chicken satay.

Preparation time: 10 MINUTES, PLUS 6 HOURS FOR MARINATING
Cooking time: 5 MINUTES
Makes 6 TO 8 SERVINGS

Marinade

1/4 cup (65 ml) fish sauce
1/4 cup (65 ml) condensed milk
3 tablespoons palm sugar
2 tablespoons sweet soy sauce
2 tablespoons vegetable oil
2 tablespoons curry powder
1 tablespoon cornstarch or tapioca
   flour
2 teaspoons ground turmeric
1 teaspoon salt
1 teaspoon ground white pepper

Chicken

2 lbs (900 g) chicken breast meat,
   sliced into 4-in x 1-in (10-cm x
   2.5-cm) strips
20 bamboo skewers, 7-in to 8-in
   (18-cm to 20-cm) long, soaked
   in cold water for 1 hour
1/2 cup (125 ml) coconut milk for
   brushing while cooking

1 Combine marinade ingredients together in a bowl. Add the chicken strips, mix well, cover and marinate overnight in the refrigerator.
2 One hour in advance, soak bamboo skewers in cold water.
3 Prepare a gas or charcoal grill. Thread each skewer with a strip of chicken, making sure that the meat lies flat and is skewered through the center. Brush with coconut milk and grill over medium-high heat for 8 to 10 minutes, turning once. Serve with Peanut Satay Sauce (see recipe to the right) and Sweet, Sour, Salty, and Spicy Cucumber Salad (page 65).

Peanut Satay Sauce

This recipe calls for both red curry paste and Thai chili paste, or *nam prik pao.* Both can be purchased at your local Asian market, but it is also possible to make your own; see page 23 for Red Curry Paste and page 22 for Thai Chili Paste. Leftover Peanut Satay Sauce can be kept in the refrigerator for up to one month. Be sure to bring it to room temperature before serving.

Preparation time: 10 MINUTES
Cooking time: 7 MINUTES
Makes 6 TO 8 SERVINGS

2 cups (500 ml) coconut milk
1/2 cup (100 g) Crispy Shallots (page 26)
1/2 cup (125 g) finely ground roasted
   peanuts
1/4 cup (65 g) palm sugar
1/4 cup (60 ml) Tamarind Juice (page 20)
2 tablespoons Red Curry Paste (page 23)
2 tablespoons Thai Chili Paste (*nam prik
   pao,* page 22)
2 tablespoons fish sauce
1 teaspoon salt

Heat the coconut milk in a saucepan over medium heat until it begins to boil. Reduce the heat to medium-low. Add remaining ingredients. Continue to cook, stirring constantly, until the sugar is dissolved and the sauce starts to bubble and thicken. Serve with the satay.

Chicken Wrapped in Pandan Leaves

Gai Hoh Bai Toey

This dish is not commonly served in Thai restaurants in Bangkok, but you can find it in Thai-Chinese restaurants there. This Thai finger food is fun to make and delicious to eat. The pandan leaf traps the juices from the chicken, making the meat extremely tender and juicy, and imparts a wonderful fragrance as well. Note that the pandan leaves are not edible. Diners should be cautioned to remove the chicken piece from the wrapping before dipping it into the Sweet and Hot sauce and enjoying it.

Preparation time: 40 MINUTES, PLUS 1 HOUR FOR MARINATING
Cooking time: 5 MINUTES
Makes 4 SERVINGS

Chicken

1 lb (500 g) boneless, skinless chicken breast meat, cut into sixteen 2 x 2 x 1/2-in (5 x 5 x 1-cm) slices
1 tablespoon Thai Pesto Paste (page 24)
16 pandan leaves, the wider the better
2 cups (500 ml) vegetable oil for deep-frying
Shredded carrots for garnish (optional)

Marinade Sauce

1 tablespoon oyster sauce
1 tablespoon soy sauce
1 tablespoon fish sauce
1 tablespoon rice wine (optional)
1 tablespoon sesame oil
1 tablespoon tapioca flour
1 tablespoon white sesame seeds
Sweet and Hot Sauce (page 25)

Pandan leaf wrap

1 Start with a rectangular piece of the pandan leaf about 12 inches long. Very long leaves may be cut in half on the diagonal. One end of the leaf should be slightly narrower than the other; leaves should be trimmed if necessary.

2 Fold the broad end of the leaf over to make a cone-like shape with a one-inch hole at the bottom; the long piece of leaf is underneath. Insert one piece of marinated chicken inside the cone.

3 Cover by inserting the long end of the pandan leaf into the top of the cone. Gently pull both ends of the pandan leaf so that most of the chicken is inside; this serves as a pocket for the chicken.

4 Don't worry if a small amount of the chicken is outside the wrapper. Trim both ends of the leaf so that they are uniform in length.

1 Place the chicken pieces in a bowl, add the Thai pesto, and mix well.

2 Combine all marinade ingredients and stir well. Add the chicken, mix by hand, and allow to marinate for at least 1 hour. Wrap each piece of chicken in a pandan leaf as described above.

3 In a deep saucepan, heat the 2 cups of oil to 350°F (175°C). Carefully add the wrapped chicken pieces to the oil and fry for about 4 minutes, or until golden; do not overcrowd the pan. Remove with a slotted spoon and drain on paper towels before serving.

4 To serve, place wrapped chicken on a serving dish and serve with the Sweet and Hot Sauce.

Thai Quesadillas

Poh Pia Kung

Once a year I run away from cold weather in the United States to visit friends and family in Thailand. During my three-month stay, we all eat out every day, looking for interesting, delicious, and—with luck—new culinary discoveries. I discovered this dish on one of my visits, adopted from a well-known foreign recipe and recreated with uniquely Thai ingredients. Perhaps it was developed to please expatriates and remind them of home.

Preparation time: 15 MINUTES, PLUS 1 HOUR FOR MARINATING
Cooking time: 10 TO 15 MINUTES
Makes 4 TO 6 SERVINGS

1 tablespoon Thai Pesto Paste (page 24)
1/2 cup (100 g) ground pork or chicken
1/2 cup (100 g) ground shrimp
1 tablespoon tapioca flour or cornstarch
1/4 cup (60 ml) vegetable oil
Six 8-in (20-cm) round spring roll wrappers
1 large egg, beaten
1/3 cup (90 ml) Sweet and Hot Sauce for dipping (page 25)
1/4 pineapple, peeled and cut into small pieces

1 Put the Thai Pesto into a large mixing bowl. Add the ground pork, shrimp, and tapioca flour; beat well. Refrigerate for at least 1 hour.
2 Heat 1/4 cup oil in a nonstick skillet over low heat. Divide the pork and shrimp mixture into 3 equal portions. Place 1 spring roll wrapper on a cutting board and spread the meat mixture evenly over the surface, leaving about 1/2 in (12 mm) of space around the edges. Use a fingertip or a brush to paint the edge of the wrapper with the beaten egg. Place the second wrapper on top, pressing down to seal the edges shut.
3 Raise the heat to medium and pan-fry the "quesadilla" until the edges turn brown, about 7 minutes. Flip over and cook the second side until golden brown, another 5 minutes. Repeat with the remaining ingredients.
4 Cut quesadillas into quarters. Serve as an appetizer with Sweet and Hot Sauce and fresh pineapple pieces.

Grilled Pork Skewers

Muu Yang

In Thailand, *Muu Yang* is as popular as grilled chicken on the street, at food markets, or near movie theaters. The seasoning may be different from one vendor to another, but each version of this dish has a sweet taste. Most Thais like to have steamed sticky rice (see page 27) along with their grilled pork.

Preparation time: 15 MINUTES, PLUS 1 HOUR
FOR MARINATING
Cooking time: 10 MINUTES, IF GRILLED
Makes 6 TO 8 SERVINGS

Marinade

6 fresh coriander roots, chopped
2 tablespoons soy sauce
2 tablespoons sweet soy sauce
2 tablespoons palm sugar
2 tablespoons fish sauce
$1/2$ cup (125 ml) coconut milk (optional)
2 tablespoons vegetable oil
$1/2$ teaspoon white peppercorns

Pork

2 lbs (900 g) pork tenderloin, sliced into
$1/2$-in x 4-in (12-mm x 10-cm) strips
20 bamboo skewers, 7 to 8 in (18 to 20 cm)
long, soaked in cold water for 1 hour

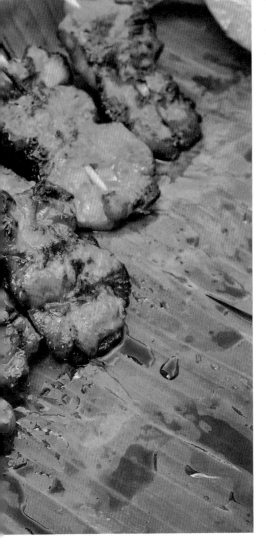

1 To make the marinade, combine the coriander roots, soy sauce, sweet soy sauce, palm sugar, fish sauce, coconut milk (if using), vegetable oil, and peppercorns in a blender and process into a fine paste. Transfer to a mixing bowl. Add the pork and marinate for at least 1 hour.

2 Prepare a gas or charcoal grill. Thread each piece of pork onto a skewer, making sure that the meat lies flat and is skewered through the center. Grill the skewers over medium-high heat for about 4 minutes on each side. Alternatively, bake the skewers at 350°F (175°C) for 35 minutes.

Thai Chicken Burgers with Thai Pesto

Burger Kai

My family was poor, and we faced tough times in the south of Thailand during and after World War II. Though meat was scarce, my mother made something she called a "pork patty" that was a special treat for the children. Sometimes I still serve it today as a sandwich filling, often substituting ground chicken for the ground pork. Thais serve this patty with steamed rice, but you can certainly put it on a hamburger bun with lettuce and tomato if you like. The patties can be prepared ahead of time and cooked just before serving. You may also substitute ground beef or pork for the chicken. For an added treat, try topping the patty with a dollop of Peanut Satay Sauce (page 35).

Preparation time: 5 MINUTES, PLUS 1 HOUR FOR MARINATING
Cooking time: 10 MINUTES
Makes 4 SERVINGS

Seasoning Sauce
1 tablespoon fish sauce
1 tablespoon soy sauce
1/4 teaspoon salt
1 tablespoon Thai Pesto Paste (page 24)

Chicken Burgers
1 lb (500 g) lean ground chicken
1 tablespoon vegetable oil
4 hamburger buns
1 cucumber, sliced
1 tomato, sliced
1 or more stems fresh coriander leaves for garnish

1 To make the seasoning sauce, mix together the fish sauce, soy sauce, and salt. Stir in the Thai Pesto. Combine this with the meat, mixing until well blended. Refrigerate for at least 1 hour.

2 To prepare the patties, shape the meat into four 1-in (2.25-cm) thick patties. Heat a large wok or skillet over medium heat until hot. Add the oil and pan-fry the patties until brown on one side, about 5 minutes. Turn the patties over and cook the other side until brown, 4 or 5 minutes more.

3 To serve, arrange the patties on the buns and top with the tomato and cucumber slices and a sprinkling of fresh coriander leaves.

Thai Shrimp Cakes

Tod Mun Kung

A popular Thai-Chinese dish served in Bangkok restaurants, shrimp cakes are an upscale version of the more commonplace fish cakes, or *tod mun pla*, a snack offered by most street vendors. Many restaurants like to serve these with fresh pineapple to offset the oily taste. Maggi seasoning sauce, which originated in Switzerland, is very popular in Thailand and is frequently found in Thai recipes. Its flavor is similar to an East Asian soy sauce, but more intense. Made from hydrolyzed vegetable protein, it contains wheat and has a small amount of naturally occurring MSG. Serve the shrimp cakes with Sweet, Sour, Salty, and Spicy Cucumber Salad (page 65) or fresh pineapple pieces.

Preparation time: 20 MINUTES, PLUS 15 MINUTES FOR CHILLING
Cooking time: 15 MINUTES
Makes 4 TO 6 SERVINGS

1 lb (500 g) shrimp, any size, peeled and deveined
1 tablespoon cornstarch
1 tablespoon fish sauce
1 tablespoon Maggi seasoning sauce or light soy sauce
1 tablespoon sesame oil
1 tablespoon granulated sugar
1 egg white
$\frac{1}{2}$ teaspoon salt
$\frac{1}{4}$ teaspoon freshly ground white pepper
1 cup (120 g) panko bread crumbs
3 cups (750 ml) vegetable oil for deep frying

1 Spread the shrimp on a plate and chill in the freezer for 15 minutes. This helps the mixture coat the patties better. Put the shrimp into a food processor. Add the cornstarch, fish sauce, Maggi seasoning, sesame oil, sugar, egg white, salt, and white pepper. Process until smooth, about 30 seconds. Transfer the mixture to a bowl.
2 Line a baking sheet with the panko breadcrumbs. Wet one hand, pick up about $\frac{1}{4}$ cup shrimp mixture, and roll it into a ball. Form into a $\frac{3}{4}$-inch (2-cm) thick patty. Place on the tray and repeat the process until the entire mixture is used up.
3 Heat the oil in a wok to 350°F (175°C) and fry the shrimp cakes, turning so they become golden brown all over, until cooked through, 2 to 3 minutes on each side. Drain on paper towels and transfer to a serving dish.

Grilled Beef with Roasted Rice Powder Dipping Sauce _Sya Rong Hai_

There are several different legends recounting how this popular Thai appetizer, often served in local Thai bars, got its unusual nickname—_Sya_ (meaning "tiger") _Rong Hai_ ("is crying"). According to one tale, the sauce is so loaded with chilies that the heat causes even tigers to cry. Another story goes that this dish was originally made with such tough beef that even tigers cried trying to eat it. Generally, the meat is cooked over a wood or charcoal fire, but a gas grill works just as well. Note that most Thais prefer their meat well done. My version, a popular special at the restaurant, packs lots of flavor, but is tender and doesn't need to be accompanied by an alcoholic beverage. We serve it as a main course with rice and a salad. I suggest using a cut of beef with a little fat; flank steak is a good choice.

Preparation time: 15 MINUTES, PLUS 4 HOURS FOR MARINATING
Cooking time: 10 MINUTES
Makes 4 TO 6 SERVINGS

Beef & Marinade

2 lbs (900 g) beef in one piece
2 cloves garlic, peeled and finely chopped
2 tablespoons soy sauce
1 tablespoon fish sauce
1 tablespoon oyster sauce
1 tablespoon vegetable oil
1/2 teaspoon freshly ground black pepper

Dipping Sauce

1/2 cup (125 ml) fish sauce
1/2 cup (125 ml) fresh lime juice
1/4 cup (65 ml) water
1 shallot, peeled and thinly sliced
2 tablespoons toasted rice powder (see page 21)
1 tablespoon chopped mint
1 tablespoon chopped fresh coriander
1 tablespoon thinly sliced green onion (scallion)
2 teaspoons ground chilies, or to taste
1 teaspoon granulated sugar

1 Place the beef into a large mixing bowl and add the remaining marinade ingredients. Let the meat marinate for about 4 hours or overnight in the refrigerator.
2 Combine all dipping sauce ingredients in a bowl. Mix well and set aside.
3 Prepare a gas or charcoal fire. Grill the meat over a hot fire until just done, about 5 minutes on each side for medium. Let the meat rest for 5 minutes before slicing. Slice the meat against the grain and arrange attractively on a serving platter. For maximum enjoyment, pass the meat with the dipping sauce.

Peanut Wafers
Tua Tod

These make a wonderful after-school snack. They also go well with drinks at a cocktail party or with beer. Growing up in the south of Thailand, I remember these wafers being sold from a glass jar in small coffee shops. Sadly, they are hard to find these days, a casualty of overwhelming competition from the heavily advertised global junk-food snack industry.

Preparation time: 5 MINUTES
Cooking time: 20 MINUTES
Makes ABOUT 12 PIECES

1 cup (250 ml) coconut milk
1 cup (240 g) unsalted peanuts, roasted
1 garlic clove, peeled and finely chopped
1 small onion, peeled and finely chopped
1/2 cup (50 g) rice flour
2 tablespoons ground toasted rice (see page 21)
1 teaspoon ground toasted coriander seeds
1/2 teaspoon salt
1/2 teaspoon ground cumin
1/4 teaspoon ground turmeric
1/4 teaspoon baking powder
3 cups (750 ml) vegetable oil for frying

1 Combine all ingredients, except for the oil, in a bowl, stirring well to blend. Set aside.
2 Heat the oil to 350°F (175°C) in a large skillet over medium heat. Carefully spoon batter 1 heaping tablespoon at a time into the hot oil; do not overcrowd the skillet. Fry the wafers until golden brown on both sides. Using a slotted spoon, remove them from the oil and drain on paper towels over a wire rack; this way the wafers retain their crispness for a few hours. Repeat until all the batter is gone.
3 Allow wafers to cool. Store in an airtight container until ready to serve.

Chapter 2

Thai Soups

Other cultures highlight soup as a first course, and may make it an elaborate dish with numerous garnishes. Thais, on the other hand, serve their soups, whether spicy or mild, as part of the main meal. "We usually serve soup in a big bowl with all the courses, whether at home or at a restaurant," says Nongkran Daks. "The host or server hands out smaller bowls so that people can dish out the soup by themselves. That way they can take as little or as much as they wish." When children are present, the soup will be clear without chilies, containing instead mild ingredients like bean thread noodles. Whether in Thailand or abroad, probably the most famous and popular soup is *Tom Yum* (page 50).

Shrimp Soup with Coconut Milk and Thai Ginger *Tom Kha Kung*

This shrimp-based soup has a refreshing, clean lime taste. If you can find fresh galangal root, also known as Thai ginger or *kha*, it will add an appealing flavor element as well as a welcome additional vegetable. Any kind of mushroom goes well in this soup, but Thais prefer the straw mushroom, available at Asian markets in cans. I also like using oyster mushrooms.

Preparation time: 10 MINUTES
Cooking time: About 15 MINUTES
Makes 4 TO 6 SERVINGS

Soup

2 cups (500 ml) coconut milk
2 cups (500 ml) chicken stock or water
1/2 lb (250 g) fresh button mushrooms, thinly sliced
1/2 lb (250 g) shrimp, shelled and deveined

First Seasonings

2 stalks lemongrass, crushed and cut into 2-in (5-cm) long pieces
Twelve 1/8-in (3-mm) thick slices galangal (optional)
3 kaffir lime leaves, torn into small pieces
2 cloves garlic, peeled and crushed
1 teaspoon salt
1/4 teaspoon freshly ground black pepper

Second Seasonings

2 fresh green chilies, sliced (optional)
3 tablespoons fresh lime juice
2 tablespoons fish sauce
1 green onion (scallion), thinly sliced
1 sprig fresh coriander, finely chopped

1 Combine the coconut milk, chicken stock, and first seasonings in a large stockpot and bring to a boil over medium heat. Add the mushrooms and cook for 3 to 5 minutes. Add the shrimp and cook for 2 to 3 minutes more, stirring once or twice to prevent curdling.

2 Just before serving, stir the second seasonings into the soup and ladle into individual serving bowls. Serve hot.

Combining ingredients and seasonings

1 Assemble all of the ingredients and prepare them.
2 Add coconut milk to the wok or pot, followed by the chicken stock, first seasonings, and when ready, the mushrooms and shrimp.
3 Add the final group of seasoning.

Spicy Lemongrass Soup with Chicken and Mushrooms *Tom Yum Kai*

This classic soup is often featured on Thai menus. It is highly adaptable; you can easily substitute or add sliced fish, calamari, shrimp, or mussels. Adding noodles to this hot-sour soup turns it into a very satisfying meal. Galangal, also known as Thai ginger, resembles ginger root but has a noticeable different flavor. For more information, see page 16.

Preparation time: 10 MINUTES
Cooking time: ABOUT 15 MINUTES
Makes 4 SERVINGS

Seasoning Sauce

3 tablespoons fresh lime juice
2 tablespoons fish sauce
2 tablespoons Thai Chili Paste or more to taste (*nam prik pao*, page 22)
1/2 teaspoon salt

Soup

4 cups (1 liter) water or chicken stock
Six 1/8-in (3-mm) thick slices galangal
2 kaffir lime leaves, torn into small pieces
1 stalk lemongrass, crushed and cut into 2-in (5-cm) lengths
1 lb (500 g) boneless, skinless chicken breast, sliced into 2 x 1 x 1/8-in (5-cm x 2.5-cm x 3-mm) pieces
1 cup (100 g) thinly sliced fresh mushrooms
2 cherry tomatoes, halved
1 green onion (scallion), finely chopped
1 stem fresh coriander, finely chopped

1 Combine all seasoning sauce ingredients in a small bowl. Whisk to blend and set aside.

2 Heat the water or stock in a large saucepan over high heat until it boils. Add the galangal, lime leaves, and lemongrass. Return to the boil and cook for 2 to 3 minutes to allow the flavors to intensify. Remove the herbs with a slotted spoon and discard them.

3 Add the chicken meat to the broth. When the mixture comes to a boil, add the mushrooms and tomatoes, and cook 3 to 4 minutes. Remove from the heat and stir in the seasoning sauce, green onion, and fresh coriander before serving.

Chicken Noodle Soup

Kuay Tiew Nam Kai

This soup, a popular meal in a bowl, can easily feed a large crowd. Whereas Vietnamese enjoy their national soup, *pho*, for breakfast, Thais enjoy this for lunch. If you use dried noodles, soften them by soaking in cold water for 1 hour before use. Then blanch them in boiling water for 1 minute, or until soft but not mushy. Fresh noodles can be used without cooking.

Preparation time: 10 MINUTES, PLUS 1 HOUR FOR SOAKING DRIED NOODLES, IF USING
Cooking time: ABOUT 1 HOUR
Makes 4 TO 6 SERVINGS

Soup

One 4- to 5-lb (1.8-kg to 2.5-kg) roasting chicken
3 qt (3.25 liters) chicken stock or water
One 2-in (5-cm) stick cinnamon
4 green onions (scallions)
One 1-in (2.5-cm) piece fresh ginger, crushed
2 teaspoons granulated sugar
2 teaspoons salt
4 tablespoons fish sauce
4 tablespoons light soy sauce

Toppings

1 lb (500 g) fresh rice noodles or 8 oz (225 g) dried rice stick noodles
1 lb (500 g) fresh bean sprouts, blanched and drained
1 bunch green onions (scallions), thinly sliced
4 sprigs fresh coriander, coarsely chopped
1/2 cup (100 g) Crispy Garlic (optional—page 26)

1 Soak the dried rice noodles for 1 hour, if using. If using fresh noodles, blanch them. Portion them equally into individual bowls, and set aside.

2 Place the whole chicken in a large stockpot and add the chicken stock or water, cinnamon, green onions, ginger, sugar, and salt. Bring to a boil over medium heat, then reduce the heat to medium-low and cook for about 1 hour. Add the fish sauce and soy sauce and remove from the heat. Set aside until ready to serve. Remove the chicken and let it cool. Bone and shred the meat.

3 Before serving, reheat the stock if it has cooled. To individual soup bowls, add a handful of noodles, bean sprouts, and shredded chicken. Ladle hot stock over the contents of the bowls. Top with sliced green onions, fresh coriander and 1 teaspoon crispy garlic, if desired.

Spicy Lemongrass Soup with Salmon and Mushrooms *Tom Yum Pla Salmon*

Once a lone customer came into my restaurant and told me that he had never eaten Thai food before. He asked me to recommend a dish, especially something with tomato in it. I thought if he wanted a tomato dish, he should go to the Italian restaurant nearby! Anyway, I fixed him this soup and he loved it, even though it only had one piece of tomato in it.

Preparation time: 5 MINUTES
Cooking time: 10 MINUTES
Makes 2 SERVINGS

1 Bring the water to a boil in a large saucepan over high heat. Add the lemongrass, galangal and lime leaves. Return to the boil, reduce the heat to medium, and continue to simmer so the herb flavors infuse the water, 2 to 3 minutes. Meanwhile, whisk the seasoning sauce ingredients together in a small bowl and set aside.

2 Remove the herbs from the broth with a slotted spoon and discard. Add the salmon, mushrooms, and tomatoes, and cook for 3 to 4 minutes or until it comes to a boil. Remove from the heat and add the seasoning sauce, green onion, and coriander. Serve hot.

Soup
3 cups (750 ml) water
1 stalk lemongrass, crushed and cut into 2-in (5-cm) sections
Six 1/8-in (3-mm) thick slices galangal
2 kaffir lime leaves, torn into small pieces
1/2 lb (250 g) salmon fillet, cut into 1-in x 2-in x 1/3-in (2.5-cm x 5-cm x 8-mm) slices
1/2 cup (50 g) thinly sliced fresh button mushrooms
2 cherry tomatoes, halved
1 green onion (scallion), thinly sliced
1 sprig fresh coriander, finely chopped

Seasoning Sauce
2 tablespoons fish sauce
2 tablespoons fresh lime juice
1 tablespoon Thai Chili Paste (*nam prik pao*, page 22)

Winter Melon Soup

Kang Jyd Fak

Winter melon, also called ash gourd, is a popular vegetable in Thailand and China, so it should be easy to find in Asian markets. It is often touted for its health-giving benefits, such as fighting edema and ulcers. If winter melon is not available, zucchini or cucumber may be used instead. Yellow bean sauce, or *tao jiao*, made from fermented yellow soy beans, is intensely salty. It is used in sauces and soups, and it normally indicates a dish with Chinese origins. Traditionally, this soup is served with Chicken Rice (*Khao Man Kai*, page 122).

Preparation time: 10 MINUTES
Cooking time: ABOUT 15 MINUTES
Makes 6 TO 8 SERVINGS

4 cups (1 liter) chicken stock
1 lb (500 g) winter melon, peeled and cubed
1 tablespoon fish sauce
2 teaspoons yellow bean sauce
1 teaspoon salt
1/4 teaspoon freshly ground black pepper
2 stems fresh coriander, coarsely chopped
1 green onion (scallion), finely chopped

1 Heat the chicken stock in a large saucepan over medium heat. Add the winter melon, reduce heat to medium-low and cook until soft, about 15 minutes.

2 Add the fish sauce, yellow bean sauce, salt, and pepper. Remove from the heat. Before serving, stir in the fresh coriander and green onion.

Rice Soup with Shrimp
Khao Tom Kung

Often served for breakfast in Thailand, this nourishing soup can be cooked with chicken, pork, beef, or a combination of meat and seafood instead of a single main protein. The pickled cabbage is a Thai product known as *tang chye*. Shredded ginger may be added, to taste.

Preparation time: 15 MINUTES
Cooking time: 20 MINUTES
Makes 4 SERVINGS

Chili Vinegar
4 medium red or green chilies, thinly sliced
1/2 cup (125 ml) apple cider vinegar

Soup
6 cups (1.5 liters) chicken stock
4 cups (600 g) cooked jasmine rice
Three 1/8-in (3-mm) thick slices galangal
1 teaspoon salt
1/2 teaspoon freshly ground white pepper
1 tablespoon chopped pickled cabbage
1 lb (500 g) shrimp
1/2 cup (100 g) thinly sliced Chinese or Western celery
2 tablespoons fish sauce
2 tablespoons Crispy Garlic (page 26)
2 green onions (scallions), sliced 1/8 in (3 mm) thick
2 stems fresh coriander, coarsely chopped

1 Combine the chili slices and cider vinegar in a small bowl and stir well. Set aside.

2 Pour the stock into a large saucepan and add the rice, galangal, salt, pepper, and pickled cabbage. Cook over medium-low heat for about 10 minutes, stirring frequently to prevent the rice from burning. Increase the heat to medium, add the shrimp and continue cooking until the shrimp are opaque, about 5 minutes. Add the celery and fish sauce.

3 Ladle the soup into individual serving bowls and garnish each serving with crispy garlic, green onions, and fresh coriander. Season with chili vinegar if desired.

Chapter 3

Thai Salads

Like soups and curries, salads are often an integral part of the Thai communal meal rather than being served as a side dish. Departing from the lettuce-based Western standard, Thai salads can be made from vegetables such as watercress (see page 62), as well as from fruits such as pomelo (see page 60), pineapple, or papaya (see page 66). Thai salads also frequently include a protein source such as beef or various kinds of seafood (see page 60). Dressings may be simple—fish sauce with fresh lime juice, chilies, and garlic—or more elaborate, incorporating coconut milk, Thai chili jam, toasted coconut, or crispy shallots. A Thai salad can be substantial enough to serve as a full meal for light eaters.

Vegetable Salad with Peanut Sauce

Salat Khaak

Adapted from the famous Indonesian salad known as *gado-gado*, this Thai version originated in Southern Thailand before becoming a national favorite. This makes a spectacular luncheon or a substantial side dish with dinner. The recipe given here for peanut sauce, which is used for the dressing, makes 3 cups. Any extra can be refrigerated or frozen for use in other dishes.

Preparation time: 20 MINUTES, PLUS 20 MINUTES FOR SOAKING
Cooking time: 30 MINUTES
Makes 6 TO 8 SERVINGS

Peanut Dressing

2 dried chilies, soaked in cold water for 20 minutes
1 cup (200 g) diced shallots or yellow onion
4 garlic cloves, peeled
1/2 cup (125 ml) water
2 1/2 cups (625 ml) coconut milk
1 1/2 cups (150 g) roasted crushed peanuts
1/2 cup (100 g) palm sugar
1/2 cup (125 ml) Tamarind Juice (page 20)
2 teaspoons salt

Salad

1/2 lb (225 g) green beans, strings removed and cut into 2-in (5-cm) pieces
1 carrot, peeled and sliced crosswise
1/2 lb (225 g) fresh spinach, watercress or lettuce, washed thoroughly and dried
2 tablespoons vegetable oil
1 lb (500 g) firm bean curd
1/2 lb (225 g) bean sprouts, blanched
1/2 lb (225 g) cabbage, shredded and blanched
2 boiled potatoes, peeled and sliced
3 hard-boiled eggs, peeled and sliced
1 cucumber, sliced crosswise into rounds
8 cherry tomatoes, halved

Corn Salad

Yam Khao Phod

This salad, which Thais serve as a side dish, is a great go-to—it's easy to make and complements almost any main course offering. I recommend using fresh kernels cut from the cob when in season. Note that if you use canned coconut milk, it should be warmed in a microwave for 30 seconds and stirred well before measuring to prevent separation.

Preparation time: 5 MINUTES
Cooking time: 5 MINUTES
Makes 4 TO 6 SERVINGS

3 cups (400 g) cooked corn kernels
1/4 cup (60 ml) water
1/2 cup (25 g) unsweetened coconut flakes, toasted until golden (see page 21)
1/4 cup (30 g) dried shrimp, lightly pounded
1/4 cup (60 g) roasted peanuts, coarsely chopped
1/4 cup (60 ml) coconut milk
2 tablespoons Thai Chili Paste (*nam prik pao*, page 22)
2 tablespoons fish sauce
2 tablespoons fresh lime or lemon juice
2 teaspoons granulated sugar (optional)
2 stems fresh coriander leaves, coarsely chopped

Heat the corn kernels and water in a saucepan over medium heat, stirring to prevent burning. Remove from the heat, drain, and allow to cool. Combine all remaining ingredients in a large salad bowl. Add corn and mix well before serving.

1 To make the peanut dressing, purée the chilies, shallots, garlic, and water in a blender or food processor until smooth. Bring the coconut milk to a boil in a saucepan over medium heat, stirring occasionally. Stir in the puréed ingredients and continue cooking over medium heat until a layer of oil appears on the surface. Add the remaining ingredients, whisking to blend well. Lower the heat to medium-low and simmer for 30 minutes, stirring occasionally. Remove from heat and allow to cool before use.

2 To make the salad, boil or steam the beans and carrots until crisp-tender. Tear the greens into bite-sized pieces and chill until crisp.

3 Heat the oil in a skillet over medium heat. Pan-fry the bean curd until golden on both sides; remove from the heat and set aside. When cool enough to handle, cut the bean curd into cubes or thin slices.

4 Arrange all the components of the salad on a serving platter, alternating colors and textures, and serve with the peanut dressing on the side.

Pomelo Salad with Shrimp

Yum Som O

Pomelo, a fruit in the citrus family which is native to Southeast Asia, looks like a large grapefruit. It is usually available between October and February in well-stocked supermarkets and Asian markets in the US. You will find two varieties of pomelo: those from Florida have yellow skins and those from California look greenish.

Surprisingly, it's now easier to find the traditional sour pomelo in the United States than in Thailand, because many years ago Thai plantation owners replaced this variety with a sweeter one for export. In some recipes, grapefruit may be substituted for pomelo, but not in this one—grapefruit is too juicy and bitter. If you're going to make *Yum Som O*, keep it more or less traditional. However, if you are using a sweet pomelo, you may reduce the amount of palm sugar. Note that if you use canned coconut milk in the dressing, it should be warmed in a microwave for 30 seconds and stirred well before measuring to prevent separation.

Preparation time: 30 MINUTES
Cooking time: 2 MINUTES
Makes 4 TO 6 SERVINGS

How to peel a pomelo

1 Make an incision in the skin.
2 Use the incision to begin peeling the thick skin from the fruit.
3 Once the skin has been peeled, separate the individual sections, and peel away the thick white membranes.
4 Cut up the freshly-peeled sections into bite-size pieces prior to adding them to the salad.

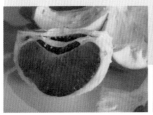

Salad
6 to 8 large shrimp, peeled and deveined
4 cups (about 600 g) peeled and seeded sour pomelo in small pieces
1/2 cup (25 g) toasted coconut flakes (see page 21)
1/2 cup (100 g) roasted cashews or peanuts
1/2 cup (100 g) Crispy Shallots (page 26)
2 tablespoons chopped fresh coriander leaves as garnish

Dressing
4 tablespoons coconut milk
4 tablespoons fresh lime juice
2 tablespoons fish sauce
2 tablespoons fresh orange juice
2 tablespoons Thai Chili Paste (*nam prik pao*, page 22)
1 tablespoon palm sugar
2 Thai hot chilies, or to taste, chopped (optional)

1 Blanch the shrimp in boiling water until cooked, about 1 minute. Drain and place in a large bowl; cover with ice to halt the cooking. Pat dry when cool.
2 Combine all dressing ingredients and whisk well to blend.
3 To serve, combine the pomelo pieces, shrimp, and dressing in a large bowl and toss well. Transfer to a serving platter and sprinkle with the toasted coconut, cashews or peanuts, crispy shallots, and chopped coriander.

Watercress Salad with Shrimp

Yum Pak Nahm

The original recipe uses water convolvulus—also called water spinach, or *pak bung* in Thai—which is only available in summertime on the east coast of the US. I have discovered, to my surprise, that substituting watercress for water convolvulus actually improves the dish. This salad requires a lot of patience, because each watercress stem must be individually deep-fried to be properly crispy and golden brown in color. My batter is a combination of wheat and rice flours, but ready-made tempura batter mix is a perfect substitute. Just follow the instructions on the package.

The dressing should be a blend of sour, sweet, and salty flavors. Note that if you use canned coconut milk, it should be warmed in a microwave for 30 seconds and stirred well before measuring to prevent separation.

Preparation time: 15 MINUTES
Cooking time: 25 MINUTES
Makes 4 TO 6 SERVINGS

Salad

6 shrimp, peeled and deveined
3 cups (750 ml) vegetable oil for deep-frying
1/2 bunch watercress, cleaned well
1/2 cup (100 g) thinly sliced red onion
2 tablespoons coarsely chopped fresh
    coriander leaves for garnish

Dressing

3 tablespoons coconut milk
3 tablespoons fresh lime juice
2 tablespoons Thai Chili Paste (*nam prik pao*,
    page 22)
2 tablespoons granulated sugar
2 tablespoons fish sauce

Batter

1 1/2 cups (375 ml) cold water
1 cup (125 g) all-purpose flour
1/2 cup (60 g) rice flour
1/2 teaspoon salt
1/2 teaspoon baking powder

1 Blanch the shrimp in boiling water until cooked, about 1 minute. Drain and place in a large bowl; cover with ice to halt the cooking. Pat dry when cool.

2 Whisk together all salad dressing ingredients until well blended. Add the shrimp to the dressing and set aside.

3 Combine all batter ingredients and mix until smooth and totally lump-free. Refrigerate until ready to use.

4 In a large wok or deep saucepan over medium heat, bring the 3 cups oil to 350°F (175°C). Dip one piece of watercress at a time into the batter, shaking off excess. Fry in the oil until golden brown and drain on a paper towel until cool. Repeat with each stem of watercress, being careful not to crowd the pan.

5 Arrange the fried watercress on a serving platter and top with the sliced red onions. Add the cooked shrimp. Pour the dressing over the salad or serve alongside. Garnish with the fresh coriander leaves.

Deep-frying battered watercress

1 Pinch off the old stems and discard.

2 Dip the watercress stems into the batter.

3 Deep-fry stems one at a time, and set aside in a clump.

4 Assemble the watercress on the plate when ready to serve.

Eggplant Salad

Yam Makhua Yaaw

For this simple salad, use slender Asian eggplants for the best flavor; these are readily available in most well-stocked supermarkets and in Asian markets. This is an ideal dish for dieters, as it has very few calories. You may wish to arrange hard-boiled egg slices around the eggplant on the platter for extra protein and a decorative touch; if so, prepare double the amount of dressing. The salad can be dressed up further by placing a few boiled shrimp on top.

Preparation time: 5 MINUTES
Cooking time: 15 MINUTES
Makes 2 SERVINGS

Dressing
2 tablespoons fresh lime juice
1¹/₂ tablespoons fish sauce
2 teaspoons granulated sugar

Salad
1 lb (500 g) Asian eggplant (about 3 eggplants)
¹/₂ red onion, thinly sliced crosswise
3 large shrimp, peeled and cooked, for garnish (optional)
2 small Thai red chilies, thinly sliced (optional)
1 tablespoon dried shrimp, soaked 10 minutes and coarsely chopped (optional)
2 to 3 hard-boiled eggs, peeled and thinly sliced (optional)
2 stems fresh coriander, coarsely chopped, for garnish

1 Whisk all dressing ingredients together and set aside.
2 Slash the skin of the eggplants lengthwise with the tip of a knife and grill or broil them until soft, about 10 minutes. Peel the eggplants by holding the cap end, pinching the skin, and pulling downwards. Cut each eggplant crosswise into 1-inch (2.5-cm) pieces and arrange on the serving dish.
3 Sprinkle the sliced onion on top of the eggplant. Garnish with the cooked shrimp, chilies, and dried shrimp, if using. Line the serving platter with the egg slices, if desired, and scatter the fresh coriander over all. Stir the dressing and pour over the salad. Serve at room temperature.

Sweet, Sour, Salty, and Spicy Cucumber Salad *Yam Tangkwa*

Like Thai cuisine as a whole, Thai salads often embody the four essential flavor profiles. This is a perfect example: it's sweet, sour, salty, and spicy all at the same time. It makes an ideal accompaniment to heavy entrées such as shrimp cakes or curries, because it counteracts the richness of these foods. This delicious salad makes a delightful accent for any meal, but should always be served in small portions alongside a satay or with shrimp or fish cakes.

Preparation time: 10 MINUTES
Cooking time: ABOUT 15 MINUTES
Makes 6 SERVINGS

½ cup (125 ml) apple cider vinegar
½ cup (100 g) granulated sugar
1 teaspoon salt
1 lb (500 g) cucumbers, peeled
2 shallots, peeled and thinly sliced crosswise
1 fresh Thai red chili, diced
2 stems fresh coriander, thoroughly chopped
2 tablespoons peanuts (optional)

1 Combine the vinegar, sugar, and salt in a small pan and bring to a boil over medium heat. Simmer, stirring, for about 5 minutes, or until the mixture becomes a thin syrup. Set aside to cool.

2 Halve each cucumber lengthwise, then cut crosswise into ¼-in (6-mm) thick slices. Combine the cucumber slices, shallots, and diced chili in a large bowl. Sprinkle with the fresh coriander. Add the peanuts, if using, and pour cooled vinegar mixture over all. Toss well and serve.

Green Papaya Salad *Som Tam*

This popular salad comes in two different versions. The first, the traditional one known as *Som Tam Lao,* originated in the northeast of Thailand and was greatly influenced by its Laotian neighbors. The green papaya salad in this book, however, hails from Bangkok; it is slightly sweeter than the northeastern one. Both versions are generally served with barbecued chicken and steamed sticky rice. Green papayas are a different variety from the typical orange-colored ones. As they are not particularly sweet, they adapt well to savory foods. Green papayas are sold year-round at Asian markets. If they are unavailable, green cabbage is an acceptable substitute.

Preparation time: 15 MINUTES, PLUS 20 MINUTES FOR SOAKING
Makes 6 TO 8 SERVINGS

Seasoning Sauce
3 tablespoons fish sauce
2 tablespoons palm sugar
2 tablespoons fresh lime juice
1 tablespoon Tamarind Juice (page 20)

Salad
7 whole black peppercorns
3 garlic cloves, peeled and finely chopped
2 dried chilies, soaked in cold water for 20 minutes
6 cups (800 g) shredded green papaya, or 5 cups (650 g) shredded cabbage plus 1 cup (150 g) shredded carrot
1 tomato, cored and cut into 8 wedges
2 tablespoons dried shrimp, crushed slightly with mortar and pestle
2 tablespoons diced fresh lime or lemon
2 tablespoons fresh lime or lemon juice
2 tablespoons crushed roasted peanuts

1 Combine all seasoning sauce ingredients in a bowl. Whisk to blend and set aside.

2 Pound the peppercorns, garlic and chilies together in a mortar and pestle until fine. Place in a small saucepan, stir in the seasoning sauce, and cook over low heat until the mixture boils. Remove from the heat and set aside.

3 Pound the papaya shreds in a mortar and pestle until they are bruised. Add the tomato and pound 3 or 4 times more, stirring the mixture as you work. Add the seasoning mixture, dried shrimp, diced limes or lemons, and juice, and stir well to combine all flavors. Arrange on a serving platter and garnish with the roasted peanuts.

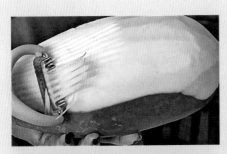

Using a mortar and pestle to prepare ingredients

1 Peel and grate the green papaya.

2 Assemble all the ingredients.

3 Gently pound the ingredients in a large serving bowl.

4 Turn the ingredients over with a large spoon while adding the seasoning sauce.

Chapter 4

Thai Poultry, Meat and Seafood

Most Thais are meat-eaters, preferring pork above all else, with chicken a close second. Duck is also popular, especially in Chinese communities. In the south of Thailand, which has a large Muslim population, as well as in the north and northeast, beef is widely eaten. In fact, Korat, the gateway to northeast Thailand, has become a major area for raising beef and dairy cattle.

Because of their proximity to both the Andaman Sea and the Gulf of Thailand, people in southern and central Thailand are particularly fond of seafood. "When I was growing up," says Nongkran Daks, "seafood was cheaper to eat than chicken or beef." Despite the dramatic increase in prices, southern Thais still love seafood.

Many Thais are not affluent, and they generally cut meat and seafood up into small pieces before cooking. If combined with vegetables and served beside rice, a little meat can go a long way.

Chiang Mai Spicy Pork Dip with Vegetables _Nam Prik Ong_

Nam Prik Ong comes from Burma originally, but it crossed the border of northern Thailand and has become a specialty in the town of Chiang Mai. This dish is traditionally served with pork rind (available in Asian and Latino markets), fresh and steamed vegetables, and steamed sticky rice.

Seasoning Sauce
2 tablespoons palm sugar
2 tablespoons fish sauce
2 tablespoons fresh lime juice

Spicy Pork Mixture
1/4 cup (50 g) chopped shallots
5 dried chilies, soaked in cold water for 20 minutes
5 garlic cloves, peeled and chopped
1 tablespoon chopped lemongrass
1 teaspoon shrimp paste
1 teaspoon salt
2 tablespoons vegetable oil
8 oz (225 g) ground pork
1 cup (200 g) sliced cherry tomatoes
1 stem fresh coriander, coarsely chopped
1 green onion (scallion), thinly sliced

Vegetables
Sliced raw cabbage, string beans, cucumber, Thai round eggplants, and pork rind in any amount to serve alongside.

Preparation time: 10 MINUTES, PLUS 20 MINUTES FOR SOAKING
Cooking time: 15 MINUTES
Makes 2 TO 4 SERVINGS

1 Combine all seasoning sauce ingredients in a small bowl. Whisk to blend and set aside.
2 Purée the shallots, chilies, garlic, lemongrass, shrimp paste, and salt in a blender or food processor. Set aside.
3 Heat the oil in a large wok over medium heat. Add the shallot mixture and stir for a few minutes until aromatic. Add the pork and the tomatoes and cook until thick, about 15 minutes. Add the seasoning sauce and stir to combine. Stir in the fresh coriander and green onion. Serve hot with the cut-up fresh vegetables.

Crispy Mussel Pancakes

Hoi Todd

This delicious street food, usually sold by pushcart vendors, is easy to find throughout Thailand between lunchtime and late in the evening, often wherever pad Thai is served. The shelled mussels are fried with scrambled eggs in a flat-bottomed pan. Thais rarely cook this dish at home, but Westerners will find it simple to prepare in their own kitchens. Gluten-free tapioca starch is often used in Thailand as a thickener. The product is sold at all Asian markets and online. If you cannot find it, you may use the same amount of store-bought tempura batter instead. For the traditional Thai taste, serve with the original Sriracha chili sauce made in Thailand or my homemade version (see page 25).

Preparation time: 15 MINUTES
Cooking time: 35 MINUTES
Makes 4 PANCAKES

Batter

1 cup (50 g) tapioca starch or cornstarch
$1\frac{1}{2}$ cups (375 ml) water
$\frac{1}{2}$ cup (65 g) all-purpose flour
1 large egg, beaten
2 tablespoons fish sauce
1 tablespoon granulated sugar
1 teaspoon baking powder
1 teaspoon salt
1 cup (200 g) uncooked shucked mussel or oyster meat

Filling

$\frac{1}{2}$ cup (125 ml) vegetable oil for frying (2 tablespoons for each pancake)
4 large eggs, each one beaten slightly and placed in a separate bowl
2 cups (250 g) bean sprouts
1 green onion (scallion), thinly sliced
4 tablespoons coarsely chopped fresh coriander leaves
1 teaspoon freshly ground black pepper

1 Combine all batter ingredients except for the mussel or oyster meat. Mix well. Divide into 4 portions and add $\frac{1}{4}$ cup (50 g) mussel or oyster meat to each portion.

2 Heat a large nonstick or cast-iron skillet over medium heat. Add 2 tablespoons oil. When the oil is hot, add one portion of the batter and cook over medium heat until the pancake begins to brown around the edges, about 5 minutes.

3 Add one slightly beaten egg to the mixture. Flip to cook the other side and fry until the egg is light brown, 3 to 5 minutes. Break the pancake into pieces with a spatula. Add $\frac{1}{2}$ cup bean sprouts and 1 tablespoon green onion and stir well. Transfer to a serving platter and sprinkle with the coriander and pepper. Repeat with the remaining portions of batter.

Grilled Chicken *Kai Yang*

There are many versions of Thai grilled chicken; they are all delicious. This recipe uses coconut milk, which is added to many dishes in the south. Traditionally, Kai Yang is served with steamed sticky rice and Green Papaya Salad (*Som Tam*, page 66). This combination of dishes originated in northeastern Thailand, where sticky rice is the preferred starch. Its popularity has spread across the country, in part because of the broad relocation of migrant workers from the northeast. If you are looking for a delicious casual dish, this makes a great picnic item.

Preparation time: 5 MINUTES, PLUS 4 HOURS FOR MARINATING
Cooking time: 30 TO 45 MINUTES
Makes 6 TO 8 SERVINGS

1/2 cup (125 ml) coconut milk
2 tablespoons dark soy sauce
2 tablespoons palm sugar
1 tablespoon fish sauce
2 teaspoons ground turmeric
2 teaspoons salt
1 teaspoon ground black pepper
2 tablespoons finely chopped fresh
   coriander stems
6 lbs (2.75 kg) chicken pieces

1 Combine the coconut milk, soy sauce, palm sugar, fish sauce, turmeric, salt, pepper and coriander stems in a large, nonreactive pan and mix well. Marinate the chicken in the mixture for at least 4 hours or overnight.
2 To prepare, light a charcoal or gas grill, and grill the chicken over medium heat until done, about 15 minutes on each side. Alternatively, bake the chicken in an oven preheated to 300°F (150°C) for 45 minutes, or until the skin is golden and the chicken is cooked through.

Stir-Fried Chinese Okra with Shrimp and Eggs *Pad Buab Kap Kung*

In spite of its name, Chinese okra is not at all like the okra found in the West; it is really a member of the cucumber family and is known commonly in Asia as "luffa." A versatile vegetable, it adapts easily to stir-frying, baking, and purée-ing. It is also delicious in soup topped with an egg. Before use, however, it is necessary to peel or scrape off the ridges on the outside of the vegetable with a vegetable peeler or knife. Chinese okra is readily available in Asian markets.

Preparation time: 5 MINUTES
Cooking time: 5 MINUTES
Makes 4 TO 6 SERVINGS

1 lb (500 g) Chinese okra
3 tablespoons vegetable oil
2 garlic cloves, peeled and minced
1/2 lb (225 g) shrimp, peeled and deveined
1/2 cup (125 ml) chicken stock or water
1 medium-sized tomato, cut lengthwise
    into 8 sections
2 tablespoons fish sauce
1 teaspoon salt
1/2 teaspoon granulated sugar
2 eggs, lightly beaten
1 green onion (scallion), chopped

1 Peel the Chinese okra, then cut using the roll-cut technique (see page 21) or slice into pieces 1/4 inch (6 mm) thick. Set aside.

2 Heat the oil in a wok over high heat. Stir-fry the garlic until golden, about 1 minute. Add the shrimp and stir-fry until they turn pink, 30 seconds to 1 minute. Add the Chinese okra and stir well.

3 Add the chicken stock, tomato, fish sauce, salt, and sugar. Cover and cook for 2 to 3 minutes. Add the eggs and green onions, stir 2 or 3 times, and cook for 1 to 2 minutes more, adding a little more chicken stock, if necessary. Remove from the heat, arrange on a platter, and serve.

Chicken with Thai Basil *Kai Pat Horapa*

This simple recipe is probably one of the most popular dishes on any Thai menu or in any Thai home. For me, the beautiful aroma of the Thai basil makes it one of my very favorite dishes. If you want it spicier, chop the hot chilies rather than slicing them; that way, more chili flavor will spread throughout the dish in the final step.

Preparation time: 5 MINUTES
Cooking time: 5 MINUTES
Makes 4 SERVINGS

Seasoning Sauce
1/4 cup (60 ml) chicken stock
2 tablespoons fish sauce
2 tablespoons oyster sauce
1 tablespoon soy sauce
1 tablespoon sweet dark soy sauce

Chicken Mixture
3 tablespoons vegetable oil
2 cloves garlic, peeled and finely chopped
1 lb (500 g) thinly sliced chicken breast
1/2 yellow onion, peeled, halved and cut lengthwise into 1/2-in (12.5-mm) slices
2 cups (200 g) thinly sliced fresh mushrooms

1 cup (130 g) cut green beans, blanched
2 green onions (scallions), cut into 1-in (2.5-cm) pieces
1 cup (30 g) fresh Thai basil leaves
3 fresh hot chilies, chopped or thinly sliced on the diagonal

1 Combine all seasoning sauce ingredients in a bowl and set aside.

2 Heat the oil in a large wok over medium heat. Add the garlic and stir-fry until it turns golden, about 3 minutes. Add the chicken and stir-fry the meat until it turns white, 2 to 3 minutes. Pour in the seasoning sauce, stirring a few times. Stir in the sliced onion, mushrooms, green beans, and green onions. Finally, add the Thai basil leaves and chilies and stir until well mixed. Serve hot.

Stir-Fried Chinese Broccoli with Crispy Pork *Pak Khanaa Muu Grob*

This fast, simple, and delicious dish can be made from any fresh vegetable, such as bean sprouts, water convolvulus, or Western broccoli. But Chinese broccoli, or *pak khanaa*, makes a perfect accompaniment for the pork. Crispy pork can be found at any Asian or Vietnamese market. Otherwise, you can make your own from thick-sliced bacon. If you choose this option, first cook the bacon until it is crisp, and add the cut-up bacon pieces to the vegetable after it is cooked.

Preparation time: 5 MINUTES
Cooking time: 5 MINUTES
Makes 2 TO 4 SERVINGS

1 lb (500 g) Chinese broccoli
3 tablespoons vegetable oil
4 garlic cloves, peeled and finely chopped
1/2 lb (250 g) crispy pork, preferably store-bought, cut into bite-sized pieces
1/4 cup (60 ml) chicken stock
1 tablespoon oyster sauce
1 tablespoon soy sauce
1 tablespoon fish sauce
1 teaspoon sugar (optional)

1 Remove the tough bottom stalk of the broccoli and discard. Peel the tough skin from the stems as well. Cut the broccoli into 2-inch (5-cm) lengths.

2 Heat the oil in a wok over medium heat. When the oil is hot, stir-fry the garlic until fragrant and golden brown. Add the pork and stir 2 or 3 times. Increase the heat to high and add the broccoli, stirring to combine thoroughly. Add the remaining ingredients. Continue cooking and stirring until all ingredients are heated through. Serve hot.

Grilled Fish Wrapped in Banana Leaves with Tamarind Dipping Sauce

Plaa Pao

Originating in my home region of southern Thailand, this recipe showcases a whole fish, with the banana-leaf wrappings adding a distinctive flavor. In its native setting, the fish is grilled outdoors, right on the white sand beaches. Coconut husks are used as fuel for the cooking fire, which adds a delectable smoky aroma. Note that banana leaves are generally sold frozen in Asian and Hispanic markets.

Preparation time: 10 MINUTES
Cooking time: 20 MINUTES
Makes 2 SERVINGS

Fish

2 tablespoons vegetable oil
1 tablespoon fish sauce
2 cloves garlic, peeled and minced
1 teaspoon freshly ground white pepper
1 teaspoon salt
One 2-lb (900-g) whole flounder or red snapper, cleaned and gutted
Banana leaves or foil for wrapping
Bamboo skewers or wooden toothpicks for securing

Tamarind Dipping Sauce

3/4 cup (180 ml) Tamarind Juice (page 20)
1/2 cup (100 g) thinly sliced shallots
1/4 cup (50 g) palm sugar
1/4 cup (60 ml) fish sauce
5 Thai chilies, chopped (optional)

1 Combine the oil, fish sauce, garlic, white pepper, and salt in a bowl. Rub the fish all over with this mixture. Wrap the fish in 4 to 5 layers of banana leaves, securing them with bamboo skewers or toothpicks. Set aside.

2 Light a gas grill or charcoal fire. When the grill is hot, cook the fish over medium-low heat for about 10 minutes on each side.

3 Meanwhile, combine all dipping sauce ingredients in a small bowl and whisk to blend. Set aside. Remove the fish from its wrapping, arrange on a platter, and serve with the dipping sauce alongside.

Stir-Fried Shrimp in Garlic Sauce

Kung Tod Kratiam Prik Thai

This dish is popular throughout Thailand. In the US, the shrimp are usually peeled, with heads removed and tails left on so that they turn a tempting dark-red color when fried. Add the optional sugar if you prefer a sweeter dish.

Preparation time: ABOUT 30 MINUTES, PLUS 1 HOUR FOR MARINATING
Cooking time: 5 MINUTES
Makes 6 TO 8 SERVINGS

2 tablespoons Thai Pesto Paste (page 24)
1 tablespoon fish sauce
1/2 cup (100 g) Crispy Garlic (page 26)
1 tablespoon light soy sauce
1 teaspoon sugar (optional)
1/2 teaspoon salt
1 lb (500 g) shrimp, shelled and deveined, with tails left on
3 tablespoons vegetable oil
1 cucumber, sliced
1 large tomato, sliced
1 stem fresh coriander, coarsely chopped for garnish

1 Put the Thai Pesto into a large bowl. Add the fish sauce, crispy garlic, soy sauce, sugar (if using), and salt. Whisk well. Add the shrimp and set aside for at least 1 hour.

2 Line a serving platter with the cucumber and tomato slices. Heat the oil in a large wok over high heat. Stir-fry the shrimp until they have turned pink, about 4 minutes. Transfer the shrimp to the serving platter and garnish with the coriander.

Three-Flavored Fish

Pla Saam Rot

Serving a whole fish always makes a lasting impression on family and friends. While Thais prefer to leave the head and tail on, this dish may also be made using fish fillets. Cooking the fish in its entirety will keep the flesh from drying out; however, to make frying easier, you can slice the fish in half crosswise and deep-fry each half separately.

Preparation time: 10 MINUTES
Cooking time: 20 MINUTES
Makes 2 SERVINGS

Seasoning Sauce

4 tablespoons granulated sugar
4 tablespoons Tamarind Juice (page 78)
3 tablespoons fish sauce
1 tablespoon oyster sauce
1 tablespoon soy sauce

Three-Flavored Fish

One 1½-lb (750-g) whole fish, such as red
   snapper, rockfish, sea bass or flounder
2 tablespoons all-purpose flour
3 cups (750 ml) vegetable oil for deep-
   frying plus 3 tablespoons
6 cloves garlic, peeled and finely chopped
6 kaffir lime leaves, shredded and separated
   into two portions
3 fresh coriander roots
2 red Thai chilies
2 green Thai chilies
¼ cup (60 ml) water
20 Thai basil leaves

1 Combine all seasoning sauce ingredients in a small bowl. Whisk to blend and set aside.

2 Rinse and dry the fish, leaving head and tail intact. Score deeply 4 to 5 times on both sides. Rub the fish inside and out with flour.

3 Heat 3 cups of oil in a wok over medium-high heat until very hot (375°F or 150°C). Carefully lower the fish into the oil and deep-fry for 10 minutes on each side until golden brown. Transfer the fish to the serving platter.

4 While the fish is frying, pound the garlic, half the kaffir lime leaves, the coriander roots, and the red and green chilies together with a mortar and pestle until roughly mixed.

5 Heat the remaining 3 tablespoons oil in a skillet over medium-high heat. Add the pounded mixture and cook, stirring, until fragrant, about 5 minutes. Stir in the seasoning sauce and cook for 2 more minutes. Add the water, the remaining kaffir lime leaves, and the Thai basil leaves, and stir. Pour the sauce mixture over the fish and serve hot.

Preparing Three-Flavored Fish

1 Score and deep-fry the fish.

2 Pound the garlic, kaffir lime leaves, coriander roots, and chilies in a mortar.

3 Stir-fry the pounded mixture in 3 tablespoons of oil.

4 Arrange the finished whole fish and top with seasoning sauce.

Steamed Fish with Lime Sauce

Pla Neung Manao

This piquant fish dish, a specialty of Central Thailand, requires a large steamer to prepare. Because it is steamed, rather than fried in oil, it is a good dish for those who are counting calories. Scoring the fish not only helps it cook more evenly, but also allows the seasoning sauce to penetrate the flesh of the cooked fish, heightening the flavor.

Preparation time: 5 MINUTES
Cooking time: 15 TO 20 MINUTES
Makes 2 TO 4 SERVINGS

Fish

One 1½-lb (750-g) whole sea bass,
  red snapper, flounder, or pompano,
  cleaned and scored on both sides
1 green onion (scallion), cut into 1-in
  (2.5-cm) long pieces
1 stem fresh coriander, coarsely chopped,
  for garnish

Lime Sauce

6 garlic cloves, peeled and coarsely
  chopped
5 fresh Thai chilies, coarsely chopped
3 tablespoons fish sauce
3 tablespoons fresh lime juice

1 Place the fish in a heat-proof serving dish and scatter the green onion pieces on top.

2 Cover the base of a large steamer with 2 inches (5 cm) of water. Place the uncovered serving dish on the steamer rack and cover the steamer. Steam for 15 to 20 minutes over high heat. Meanwhile, combine all the sauce ingredients in a bowl.

3 Remove the serving dish from the steamer. Pour the sauce over the fish and garnish with the coriander.

Stir-Fried Asparagus with Shrimp

Pad Naw Mai Farang Kap Kung

Though asparagus is native to Europe, Asia Minor, and parts of Africa, it is also grown and harvested in Thailand. Much of the crop is destined for export, but local Thai cooks enjoy it as well. They have adapted this slender stalk to a number of savory recipes, including this colorful pink-and-green dish featuring shrimp and asparagus. Asparagus stalks usually have a tough base that should be snapped off and discarded before cooking.

Preparation time: 5 MINUTES
Cooking time: 5 MINUTES
Makes 4 SERVINGS

1 lb (500 g) asparagus, cut into 2-in (5-cm) lengths
3 tablespoons vegetable oil
3 garlic cloves, peeled and finely chopped
1/2 lb (250 g) shrimp, shelled and deveined
1/2 cup (125 ml) chicken stock
2 tablespoons fish sauce

1 Blanch or steam the asparagus until just tender; plunge into cold water to stop the cooking. Drain and set aside.

2 Heat the oil in a wok over medium heat. Add the garlic and stir-fry until golden, about 3 minutes. Add the shrimp and stir-fry for 2 minutes, or until it turns pink.

3 Add the asparagus, stir well, and cover the wok for about 2 minutes. Uncover and add the chicken stock and fish sauce. Stir several times to combine thoroughly, then remove from the heat. Serve hot.

Spicy Beef with Mint Leaves

Laab Nua

This is a favorite dish in northeastern Thailand, near the Laotian border. It goes beautifully with steamed sticky rice. The flavors of the seasonings work just as well with pork, chicken, and even catfish. To be traditional and authentic, the beef must be chopped into coarse pieces by hand.

Preparation time: 7 TO 10 MINUTES
Cooking time: 5 MINUTES
Makes 4 TO 6 SERVINGS

1 lb (500 g) lean chopped or minced beef
2 cloves garlic, peeled and finely chopped
5 tablespoons fresh lime juice
3 tablespoons fish sauce
1/2 teaspoon salt
1 cup (30 g) fresh mint leaves
2 shallots, peeled and thinly sliced
2 green onions (scallions), finely chopped
2 stems fresh coriander, finely chopped
3 tablespoons toasted rice powder (see page 21)
1 teaspoon ground chili

Assorted vegetables for accompaniments:
Lettuce, cabbage, fresh Thai basil leaves, cucumber slices, and/or raw green beans

1 Heat a nonstick skillet over medium heat. Cook the meat and garlic without oil until they change color, about 7 minutes. Transfer to a mixing bowl to cool.

2 Add the lime juice, fish sauce, and salt. Mix well. Stir in the mint leaves, shallots, green onions, fresh coriander, rice powder, and ground chili, and toss to combine.

3 To serve, arrange the beef mixture on a serving platter and surround it with the accompanying vegetables.

Stewed Pork and Eggs

Muu Khai Palo

Thais usually make a big pot of this stew so they can serve it at home for several days. This is especially nice because its flavor just gets better over time. The leftover eggs are also great for breakfast or a picnic. Thais usually serve *Muu Khai Palo* with curry rather than offering it on its own. If you are serving a lot of guests, this dish is a good choice paired with any kind of Thai curry. Allow one egg and 3 to 4 pieces of pork per person. Chicken legs may be substituted for the pork if a change of pace is desired. I like to make this a day or two ahead so I can refrigerate it overnight. This makes it easy to skim the fat off the surface before reheating.

Preparation time: 10 MINUTES
Cooking time: ABOUT 50 MINUTES
Makes 6 TO 8 SERVINGS

Seasoning Sauce
1/2 cup (100 g) palm sugar
1/3 cup (95 ml) fish sauce
1 tablespoon dark soy sauce
1 teaspoon five-spice powder

Pork
1 tablespoon Thai Pesto Paste (page 24)
2 tablespoons vegetable oil
1 lb (500 g) pork butt, cut into 1-in (2.5-cm) cubes
2 cups (250 ml) water
8 hard-boiled eggs, peeled

1 Combine all seasoning sauce ingredients in a bowl and whisk to blend. Set aside.
2 Heat the oil in a large saucepan over medium heat. Add the Thai Pesto and stir-fry until fragrant, about 3 minutes. Add the pork and brown the cubes on all sides. Pour off any excess fat. Stir in the seasoning sauce and mix well. Add the water and the eggs, stir once, then cover and reduce the heat to low. Cook about 40 minutes, or until the pork is tender.

Fish Fillets with Ginger *Pla Pad Khing*

Fresh ginger and salty yellow bean sauce (*tao jiao*) make a delicious seasoning for this fish dish. This recipe works well with pork, chicken, or beef; for vegetarians, it's also delicious with bean curd. Some Thai cooks dredge the fish fillets in tapioca flour before frying; this ensures that the fillets stay in one piece and adds a crunchy texture. If you choose to do this, be sure not to overcook the fish. Dredging is not necessary for pork, chicken, or beef.

3 tablespoons vegetable oil
3 garlic cloves, peeled and finely chopped
1/2 cup (100 g) shredded fresh ginger, preferably young ginger
1 lb (500 g) white meat fish fillets, cut into bite-sized pieces
1/2 cup (125 ml) chicken stock or water
1 tablespoon yellow bean sauce
4 green onions (scallions), cut into 2-in (5-cm) pieces
2 chilies, seeded and cut into strips (optional)
1 tablespoon fish sauce
1 tablespoon soy sauce
1 teaspoon sugar
1 stem fresh coriander, coarsely chopped, for garnish

Preparation time: 5 MINUTES
Cooking time: 8 MINUTES
Makes 2 TO 4 SERVINGS

1 Heat the oil in a large wok over medium heat. Stir-fry the garlic and ginger until golden, about 3 minutes.
2 Add the fish, chicken stock, and bean sauce, stirring to combine. Cover and cook for 5 minutes.
3 Stir in the green onions, chilies (if using), fish sauce, soy sauce and sugar, mixing well. Serve hot, garnished with the fresh coriander.

Stir-Fried Shrimp and Chicken with Cashews *Kung Kai Himmapan*

I cook this dish when I crave something spicy, but feel too lazy to make curry. It's also a good way to use up any *nam prik pao* left over from making *Tom Yum Kai* soup (page 50).

Seasoning Sauce
1/2 cup (125 ml) chicken stock or water
1/4 cup (65 ml) Thai Chili Paste (*nam prik pao*, page 22)
1 tablespoon fish sauce
1 tablespoon soy sauce
1 tablespoon oyster sauce

Shrimp & Chicken Mixture
3 tablespoons vegetable oil
3 cloves garlic, peeled and finely chopped
1/2 lb (250 g) chicken breast meat, thinly sliced
1/2 small onion, peeled and sliced lengthwise
1/2 lb (250 g) shrimp, peeled and deveined
1 cup (120 g) cashews
3 green onions (scallions), cut into 1-in (2.5-cm) sections

Preparation time: 7 MINUTES
Cooking time: 5 MINUTES
Makes 4 TO 6 SERVINGS

1 Combine all seasoning sauce ingredients in a bowl. Whisk well and set aside.
2 Heat the oil in a wok over medium heat. When oil is hot, add the garlic and stir-fry until golden. Add the chicken and stir-fry until the meat turns white. Stir in the onion, then add the shrimp and stir-fry until the shrimp turns pink, about 30 seconds. Add the seasoning sauce, stir a few times, and keep over the heat until the sauce boils. Mix in the cashews and green onions and remove from heat. Transfer to a platter and serve.

Chapter 5

Thai Curries

Curries are a daily part of communal meals in southern and central Thailand. Each day's curry features a different meat or seafood combined with an array of vegetables. Always served with rice, a curry makes for a substantial main course, and the leftovers may be eaten for breakfast the following day.

"In the south," says Nongkran Daks, "seafood is plentiful, so when I was growing up, we ate fish and other seafood curries every day." Southern curries may have been introduced by Arab traders from Indonesia and Malaysia centuries ago, but Thais have developed their own versions, such as Masaman Curry (page 104) and Panang Curry (page 101). Curries in central Thailand feature coconut milk, but tend to be sweeter than southern curries. In northeastern and northern Thailand, people eat fewer curries; when they do prepare them, they do not use coconut milk. Overall, grilled foods with spicy dipping sauces and chili jams are more popular in this region. "The foods of the northeast and south are very spicy," says Nongkran. "While there are curries in Thailand that have been influenced by neighboring countries, due to creativity in adaptation these dishes are now uniquely Thai."

Green Curry with Chicken, Bamboo Shoots, and Thai Eggplant

Kang Khiew Wan Kai Kap Naw Mai

This is probably the most popular curry in all of Thailand. It owes its outstanding flavor to the classic and traditional Green Curry Paste (page 24). The success of this versatile seasoning, which goes well with seafood, meat, noodles, and bean curd, depends on the perfect combination of fresh herbs and spices. Green curry paste is easy to make at home, though it can also be purchased premade. If you make it yourself, you can intensify its green color by adding some spinach leaves; these will not affect the flavor. In Thailand, cooks use the young leaves of Thai chilies for this purpose.

Preparation time: 15 MINUTES
Cooking time: 15 MINUTES
Makes 6 TO 8 SERVINGS

2 cups (500 ml) coconut cream
1 cup (220 g) Green Curry
    Paste (page 24)
1 lb (500 g) boneless chicken
    breast, sliced into 2 x 1 x 1/8-
    in (5-cm x 2.5-cm x 3-mm)
    pieces
4 cups (400 g) cubed bamboo
    shoots and/or eggplant
2 tablespoons fish sauce
1 teaspoon palm sugar
3 kaffir lime leaves, torn into
    small pieces
20 leaves fresh Thai basil

1 Scoop out 1 cup (250 ml) coconut cream from the top of the can into a heavy saucepan and bring to a boil over medium heat, stirring occasionally. Cook for 1 to 2 minutes. Stir in the curry paste and continue cooking for 3 to 4 minutes, or until it becomes fragrant. Add the remaining 1 cup (250 ml) coconut cream.

2 Add the chicken and bring to a boil. Cover, reduce the heat to medium-low, and continue to cook until the meat is tender, 7 to 10 minutes. Add the bamboo shoots or eggplant and cook for 5 minutes more. Stir in the fish sauce, palm sugar, kaffir lime leaves, and basil leaves. When the mixture is heated through, serve with rice or noodles.

Dry Pork Curry with String Beans

Pad Prik Khing Mu Kap Tua

This is a delicious curry made without coconut milk. You can make it ahead of time and add the string beans just before serving. This curry has a strong flavor, so be sure to serve it with plenty of rice. The optional dried shrimp, a Thai staple, adds a mild, salty flavor and a chewy texture. If the dish gets too dry while cooking, add a little water, but remember that it is not supposed to be soupy.

Preparation time: 20 MINUTES, PLUS 20 MINUTES FOR SOAKING
Cooking time: 15
Makes 6 TO 8 SERVINGS

Curry Paste
- 1/4 cup (50 g) thinly sliced lemongrass
- 6 garlic cloves, peeled and chopped
- 5 whole black peppercorns
- 5 dried chilies, soaked in water for 20 minutes
- 5 shallots, peeled and quartered
- Three 1/8-in (3-mm) thick slices galangal, shredded
- 3 fresh coriander roots, coarsely chopped
- 1 teaspoon coarsely chopped kaffir lime rind
- 1 teaspoon salt
- 1 teaspoon shrimp paste
- 1/2 cup (125 ml) water, or more as needed

Pork & String Bean Mixture
- 2 tablespoons vegetable oil
- 1 lb (500 g) lean pork, cut into 2 x 1 x 1/8-in (5-cm x 2.5-cm x 3-mm) pieces
- 1/2 cup (125 ml) water
- 1/2 lb (250 g) string beans, ends removed, cut into 2-in (5-cm) long pieces, and blanched
- 3 kaffir lime leaves, shredded crosswise
- 2 tablespoons fish sauce
- 2 tablespoons dried shrimp, slightly crushed (optional)
- 1 tablespoon palm sugar

1 Combine all curry paste ingredients in a blender and blend until smooth, adding more water as needed. Set aside.

2 Heat the oil in a large wok over medium heat. Add the pork and stir-fry until it turns white, about 5 minutes. Remove and set aside. Stir in the curry paste and cook until fragrant, about 5 minutes. Return the pork to the wok and stir well to coat the meat with curry paste. Add the 1/2 cup (125 ml) water, string beans, kaffir lime leaves, fish sauce, dried shrimp (if using), and palm sugar. Stir until well combined. If the curry seems too dry, add water a little at a time, but be careful not to use too much. Remove from the heat and serve.

Pineapple Curry with Shrimp

Kang Khua Saparot Kung

In Thailand, only high-end restaurants serve this curry. It is certainly a majestic dish, especially because of its striking orange-red hue. The coconut milk adds a seductive richness. The flavor of this curry should include both sweet and sour elements. If the pineapple is on the sweet side, counterbalance by adding more lime juice.

Preparation time: 20 MINUTES, PLUS 20 MINUTES FOR SOAKING
Cooking time: 20 MINUTES
Makes 4 TO 6 SERVINGS

Curry Paste
5 dried red chilies, soaked in water for 20 minutes
5 shallots, peeled
5 garlic cloves, peeled and chopped
Three 1/8-in (3-mm) thick slices galangal, shredded
1/4 cup (50 g) thinly sliced lemongrass
3 fresh coriander roots, coarsely chopped
1 teaspoon salt
1 teaspoon shrimp paste
1/2 cup (125 ml) water, or more as needed

Seasoning Sauce
2 tablespoons fresh lime or lemon juice
1 tablespoon fish sauce
1 tablespoon sugar

Shrimp & Pineapple Mixture
Two 13.5-oz (400-ml) cans coconut milk
2 cups (250 g) cut-up fresh pineapple
1/2 lb (225 g) shrimp, shelled and deveined
3 kaffir lime leaves, shredded

1 Combine all curry paste ingredients in a blender or food processor. Purée until smooth, adding more water if necessary. Set aside.

2 Combine all seasoning sauce ingredients in a small bowl. Stir well and set aside.

3 Pour the coconut milk into a heavy saucepan and bring to a boil over medium heat, stirring occasionally. Stir in the curry paste and continue cooking for 3 to 4 minutes, or until it becomes fragrant. Add the pineapple, the shrimp, the seasoning sauce, and the lime leaves, stirring after each addition. Cook until the shrimp turn pink. Remove from the heat and serve hot.

How to select and cut a pineapple

1 Thailand may be the world's biggest grower of pineapple, producing nearly 3 million tons of this popular fruit annually. Much of the crop is shipped overseas, which means that people everywhere can enjoy Thai pineapples almost year round. It's important, however, to know how to select a pineapple that is fully ripe but not overripe. Look for pineapples that have a yellow-gold hue, especially around the base of the fruit. The skin should be firm but soft to the touch. Easily pulling a leaf from the center, or crown, of the pineapple does not ensure ripeness. Pineapples that are moldy, cracked, or too soft to the touch should be avoided.

2 Use a sharp knife to slice off the top and bottom and peel the skin. The spiral rows of "eyes" show clearly. Hold the knife at a 45-degree angle to excavate the eyes, starting at the bottom of the pineapple, and lifting out the cut portions as you follow the spiral. Repeat for all rows, quarter the pineapple, cut out the core, and slice as desired.

Roasted Duck Curry with Wild Eggplants and Tomatoes Kang Phet Ped Yang

While many kinds of curry can be bought from street vendors throughout Thailand, this Roasted Duck Curry is more upscale, as the ingredients are costly. Duck entered Thai cuisine via the Chinese, who brought it with them to ancient Siam. The old capital, Ayuthaya, is still a major poultry-raising center. Pairing roast duck with the Thai wild eggplant, however, was a Thai innovation. More recently, some Thai chefs have innovated further, adding ingredients such as fresh pineapple, green apples, and even grapes to this dish. I prefer the traditional version, however. I especially enjoy the gorgeous contrast between the red tomatoes and the green wild eggplant. Wild eggplant, sometimes called "pea eggplant," grows in bunches and looks very much like peas (see photo on page 19). If you cannot find wild or round Thai eggplant, you may substitute regular slender Asian eggplants. Most Chinese markets sell whole roast duck, but you can of course roast your own duck at home if you prefer.

Preparation time: 20 MINUTES,
PLUS 20 MINUTES FOR SOAKING
Cooking time: 15 MINUTES
Makes 6 TO 8 SERVINGS

Curry Paste
5 dried red chilies, soaked in water
    for 20 minutes
1/4 cup (50 g) thinly sliced
    lemongrass
Three 1/8-in (3-mm) thick slices
    galangal, shredded
3 fresh coriander roots
1 tablespoon toasted coriander seeds
2 teaspoons cumin seeds
1 teaspoon ground mace
1 teaspoon peppercorns
1 teaspoon coarsely chopped kaffir
    lime rind
1 teaspoon salt
1 teaspoon shrimp paste
1/4 teaspoon freshly grated nutmeg
4 garlic cloves, peeled and chopped
3 shallots, peeled and quartered
1/2 cup (125 ml) water, or more as
    needed

Duck, Eggplant & Tomato Mixture
One 13.5-oz (400-ml) can coconut milk
One 2-lb (900-g) boned roast duck, cut into bite-
    sized pieces
15 cherry tomatoes, halved
1/2 cup (100 g) Thai wild eggplant or 1 cup (200 g)
    cut-up round Thai eggplant
20 Thai basil leaves
3 kaffir lime leaves
2 tablespoons fish sauce
1 teaspoon sugar

1 Combine all curry paste ingredients in a blender or food processor. Purée until smooth, adding more water as needed. Set aside.

2 Pour the coconut milk into a heavy saucepan and bring to a boil over medium heat, stirring occasionally. Stir in the curry paste and continue cooking for 3 to 4 minutes, or until it becomes fragrant.

3 Add the roast duck pieces and bring the mixture to a boil. Reduce the heat to low, cover, and simmer until the meat is tender, about 10 minutes. Add the tomatoes and eggplant, and continue cooking for about 5 minutes more. Add the Thai basil leaves, kaffir lime leaves, fish sauce, and sugar. Stir to combine flavors thoroughly. Serve hot.

Steamed Seafood Curry *Hor Mok Talay*

The traditional preparation for *Hor Mok Talay* calls for wrapping seasoned seafood in banana leaves and cooking it in a bamboo steamer. Many modern Thai and Western cooks skip the impressive-looking banana leaf wrappings—which add a level of flavor—and use heatproof ramekins instead. Or they may skip the steaming altogether and cook the ingredients in a wok or skillet. But to achieve the subtle, eggy texture of the real *Hor Mok*, steaming is essential. If you don't have banana leaves, you can steam the seafood in red or green bell peppers and eat the whole thing. To learn how to make banana-leaf cups, see the sidebar. This dish contains rhizome, or lesser galangal, a Thai ingredient typically found only at Asian markets.

Curry Paste

1/3 cup (100 ml) water
3 dried chilies, soaked in cold water for 20 minutes
3 shallots, peeled and quartered
6 garlic cloves, peeled
Three 1/8-in (3-mm) thick slices galanagal, shredded
1/4 cup (50 g) thinly sliced lemongrass
1 teaspoon shredded kaffir lime rind
6 fresh coriander roots, coarsely chopped, or
    4 tablespoons chopped fresh coriander stems
10 whole black peppercorns
1 tablespoon chopped rhizome (see page 113)
1 teaspoon shrimp paste
1 teaspoon salt

Seafood Mixture

1 1/2 lbs (700 g) mixed peeled shrimp, calamari, fish slices, and shelled mussels
1 1/2 cups (375 ml) coconut cream
1/4 cup (60 ml) fish sauce
2 eggs, separated
4 stems fresh coriander, roughly chopped, 2 tablespoons reserved for garnish
2 cups (260 g) cut-up cabbage leaves, blanched
2 cups (60 g) fresh Thai basil leaves
1/2 cup (125 ml) coconut cream, for topping
3 kaffir lime leaves, shredded, for garnish
2 fresh red chilies, seeded and sliced, for garnish

Preparation time: 25 MINUTES, PLUS 20 MINUTES FOR SOAKING THE CHILIES
Cooking time: 25 MINUTES
Makes 6 TO 8 SERVINGS

1 Place all curry paste ingredients in a blender. Blend until smooth.

2 Combine the seafood, coconut cream, and fish sauce with the curry paste in a large mixing bowl. Stir until all the ingredients are well combined and the mixture is thick. While stirring, add the egg yolks and mix well.

3 Beat the egg whites until stiff. Fold them into the mixture, blending well. Stir in all but 2 tablespoons of the chopped fresh coriander.

4 Line 8 banana-leaf cups (or 8 ramekins, if not using banana-leaf cups) with the cabbage and basil leaves. Spoon the seafood mixture into the cups or ramekins. Steam over medium-high heat for 15 to 20 minutes. Spoon the coconut cream over top, and garnish with the remaining coriander leaves, kaffir lime leaves and chilies. Steam again for 2 minutes more. Serve hot.

Making banana-leaf cups

While you can cook Steamed Seafood Curry in a ramekin, steaming individual servings in banana leaf cups is authentic, making for an exotic presentation and imparting an even more delightful aroma to the dish. Banana leaves can be found in the freezer section of most Asian and Hispanic supermarkets.

1 Cut the banana leaves into 16 rounds, each 6 inches (15 cm) in diameter. Using a 6-inch round bowl as a guide, cut around the edges with the tip of a sharp knife.

2 Stack two rounds together. Holding the layers together, fold in the edge to create a pleat about 1 inch (2.5 cm) deep. Use a hand-held stapler to fasten the leaves together, forming a square corner.

3 Fold and staple the opposite side in the same manner. Repeat the procedure on opposite sides halfway between the first two pleats to form a square container.

Curry with Grilled Beef and Vegetables

Kang Pa Nua Yang

This dish, also known as Jungle Curry, is another delicious curry made without coconut milk. You can substitute any meat you like for the beef, but top round or flank steak is ideal. Serve this curry alongside hot rice.

Preparation time: 15 MINUTES, PLUS 20 MINUTES FOR SOAKING
Cooking time: 35 MINUTES
Makes 8 TO 10 SERVINGS

Curry Paste

2 dried red chilies, soaked in cold water for 20 minutes
2 tablespoons uncooked rice, soaked in $\frac{1}{2}$ cup (125 ml) water for 20 minutes
5 fresh Thai chilies, or to taste
5 garlic cloves, peeled and chopped
4 shallots, peeled
$\frac{1}{4}$ cup (50 g) thinly sliced lemongrass
Five $\frac{1}{8}$-in (3-mm) thick slices galangal, shredded
4 fresh coriander roots, coarsely chopped
1 teaspoon minced kaffir lime rind
1 teaspoon salt
1 teaspoon shrimp paste
$\frac{1}{2}$ teaspoon roasted coriander seeds
15 whole black peppercorns
$\frac{1}{2}$ cup (125 ml) water, or more as needed

Beef & Vegetable Mixture

1 lb (500 g) lean beef
3 tablespoons vegetable oil
6 cups (1.5 liters) water
$\frac{1}{2}$ lb (225 g) bamboo shoots, cut into 2 x 1 x $\frac{1}{8}$-in (5-cm x 2.5-cm x 3-mm) pieces
20 green beans, cut into 2-in (5-cm) lengths
1 Asian eggplant, cut into 2-in (5-cm) pieces
20 fresh Thai basil leaves
3 kaffir lime leaves, torn into small pieces
3 tablespoons fish sauce

1 Combine all curry paste ingredients in a blender. Purée until smooth, adding more water as needed. Set aside.

2 Broil the beef for 4 to 5 minutes on each side. When it is cool enough to handle, slice it into 2 x 1 x $\frac{1}{8}$-inch (5-cm x 2.5-cm x 3-mm) pieces. Set aside.

3 Heat the oil in a large saucepan over medium heat. Add the curry paste and fry until fragrant, about 3 minutes. Add the meat and stir-fry for 3 to 4 minutes. Stir in the 6 cups (1.5 liters) water, the bamboo shoots, green beans and eggplant, and cook about 5 minutes. Stir in the Thai basil leaves, kaffir lime leaves and fish sauce. Remove from the heat and serve.

Chiang Mai Pork Curry

Kang Hang Lay

A favorite dish in Northern Thailand, this curry originated in Burma. Its Burmese counterpart is served as a course in a *Khan Toke* meal, a celebratory festival that derives its name from the pedestal table on which several dishes are served for this occasion. Note that the seasonings for this unusual curry closely resemble those of Masaman Curry (page 104).

You can substitute spareribs for the pork loin, but if you do so, parboil them first to remove any impurities.

Preparation time: 15 MINUTES, PLUS 20 MINUTES FOR SOAKING AND 1 HOUR FOR MARINATING
Cooking time: 50 MINUTES
Makes 6 TO 8 SERVINGS

Curry Paste
9 dried red chilies, soaked in cold water for 20 minutes
1/4 cup (30 g) thinly sliced lemongrass
Ten 1/8-in (3-mm) thick slices galangal, shredded
1 tablespoon curry powder
1 teaspoon ground turmeric
3 shallots, peeled and quartered
6 cloves garlic, peeled and chopped
1 teaspoon shrimp paste
1 teaspoon salt
1/2 cup (125 ml) water

Pork Mixture
2 tablespoons sweet black soy sauce
3 lbs (1.5 kg) boneless pork loin, cut into 1-in (3-cm) cubes
3 tablespoons vegetable oil
5 cups (1.25 liters) water
3 plum tomatoes, each cut into eighths
1/2 cup (65 g) shredded ginger
1 cup (250 ml) Tamarind Juice (page 20)
1 cup (100 g) coarsely ground peanuts
3 tablespoons fish sauce
2 tablespoons light soy sauce
2 tablespoons palm sugar

1 Combine all curry paste ingredients in a blender and process until smooth. Pour half the curry paste into a large bowl, reserving the remaining half for later. Stir in the sweet black soy sauce and the cubed pork. Marinate the pork for at least 1 hour.

2 To make the curry, heat a large wok over medium-high heat and add the vegetable oil. When the oil is hot, add about a fourth of the marinated pork. Stir-fry until the meat changes color. Transfer the cooked meat to a large stockpot. Repeat with the remaining pork until all the meat is cooked.

3 Add the 5 cups water to the stockpot and place over high heat. Stir in the remaining half of the curry paste and cook until the mixture comes to a boil. Reduce heat to medium and add the tomatoes, ginger, tamarind juice, peanuts, fish sauce, light soy sauce, and palm sugar, stirring after each addition. Continue cooking until the meat is tender and the liquid has evaporated, about 35 minutes. Serve hot.

Panang Beef Curry

Panang Nua

This Southern Thai curry is one of my favorite dishes. It is thicker and more concentrated than most curries. It is not overly spicy, and should have a slightly sweet taste. While a chicken or beef version of this dish is most common, it can also be made as a vegetarian entrée by leaving out the meat and adding tofu.

Like most other curries, this one is traditionally served with rice, but is also delicious over pasta, and I've heard of several people who eat Panang Beef Curry with bread. You can even find some pizza places in Bangkok that use this curry as a pizza topping, which is popular with both Thais and expats.

Curry Paste

7 dried chilies, soaked in cold water for 20 minutes
Five 1/8-in (3-mm) thick slices galanagal, shredded
1/4 cup (50 g) thinly sliced lemongrass
5 shallots, peeled and quartered
7 garlic cloves, peeled
3 fresh coriander roots, chopped
1 teaspoon minced kaffir lime rind
1 teaspoon shrimp paste
1 teaspoon toasted coriander seeds
1 teaspoon salt
20 black peppercorns
1/2 cup (125 ml) water
1/4 cup (50 g) ground peanuts

Beef Mixture

2 1/2 cups (625 ml) coconut cream
2 lbs (900 g) lean beef, thinly sliced
20 fresh Thai basil leaves, plus extra for garnish
3 kaffir lime leaves, shredded crosswise, plus extra for garnish
2 red or green chilies, minced (optional), plus extra for garnish
2 tablespoons fish sauce
2 tablespoons Thai palm sugar

Preparation time: 15 MINUTES, PLUS 20 MINUTES FOR SOAKING
Cooking time: 15 MINUTES
Makes 6 TO 8 SERVINGS

1 Combine all curry paste ingredients except the peanuts in a blender. Process until smooth. Stir in the ground peanuts, blend one more time, and set aside.

2 Scoop 1 cup (250 ml) of the coconut cream into a saucepan and bring to a boil over medium heat, stirring occasionally. Stir in the curry paste and reduce the heat to medium-low; cook until the mixture is fragrant, 3 to 4 minutes.

3 Add the beef to the saucepan and stir until well mixed. Add the remaining 1½ cups (375 ml) coconut cream. Cook for about 5 minutes more, or until the meat loses its pink color. Add the Thai basil leaves, the kaffir lime leaves, chilies (if using), fish sauce, and sugar. Stir until well combined. Serve hot.

Southern Thai Chicken Curry

Kang Kai Kole

If you travel to the far south of Thailand, you might find grilled chicken with *kole* sauce, which is the curry paste featured in this recipe. You don't really have to buy curry paste because it is so easy to make from scratch. After you taste this curry, you may never want to use commercial curry paste again.

Preparation time: 25 MINUTES, PLUS 20 MINUTES FOR SOAKING
Cooking time: 1 HOUR
Makes 6 TO 8 SERVINGS

Curry Paste

1/2 cup (125 ml) water, or more as needed
12 shallots or 1 small yellow onion, peeled and diced
10 garlic cloves, peeled
7 dried red chilies, soaked in cold water for 20 minutes
1 teaspoon ground cinnamon
1 teaspoon coriander seeds
1 teaspoon cumin seeds
2 teaspoon ground turmeric
1 teaspoon shrimp paste

Seasoning Sauce

5 tablespoons Tamarind Juice (page 20)
4 tablespoons fish sauce
2 tablespoons palm sugar
1 teaspoon salt

Chicken Mixture

3 tablespoons vegetable oil
2 1/2 cups (625 ml) coconut cream
5 lbs (2.25 kg) skinless chicken breast or thigh, bone in
2 large potatoes, peeled and cubed

Making Chicken Curry

1 Assemble all the ingredients.
2 Heat the 3 tablespoons of vegetable oil in a wok and stir-fry the curry paste until fragrant.

3 Stir in the coconut milk.
4 Add the chicken pieces, and continue cooking until the chicken is done, about 40 minutes, before adding the potatoes.

1 Place all curry paste ingredients in a blender or food processor. Purée until smooth, adding extra water if needed. Set aside.

2 Combine all seasoning sauce ingredients. Whisk to blend and set aside.

3 Heat the oil over medium heat in a large, heavy pot such as a Dutch oven. Add the curry paste and stir a few times. Add the coconut cream and stir until mixture is well combined. When it comes to a boil, add the chicken, cover the pot, reduce the heat to medium-low and cook for 40 minutes, stirring occasionally. Add the potatoes and continue cooking until the chicken and potatoes are tender, about 20 minutes more. Stir in the seasoning sauce and serve.

Beef Curry with Potatoes and Peanuts *Kang Masaman Nua*

This dish is probably the most popular curry among Westerners. Since it is time-consuming to make, Thais usually reserve it for special occasions. I remember that my mother made this curry for me when I brought my foreign boyfriend (now my husband) home for the first time. This is her recipe. In the unlikely event that you have leftovers, they can be frozen. The taste should be a delicious combination of sweet, sour, and salty.

Curry Paste

7 dried chilies, soaked in cold water for 20 minutes
$1/4$ cup (50 g) thinly sliced lemongrass
Five $1/8$-in (3-mm) thick slices galanagal, shredded
3 fresh coriander roots, coarsely chopped
5 shallots, peeled and coarsely chopped
8 garlic cloves, peeled and chopped
$1/2$ whole nutmeg kernel
5 cloves
5 cardamom pods, inner seeds only
1 tablespoon coriander seeds
2 teaspoons shrimp paste
1 teaspoon cumin seeds
$1/2$ teaspoon whole black peppercorns
2 blades mace, or 1 teaspoon ground mace
$1/2$ cup (125 ml) water
1 teaspoon salt

Beef, Potato & Peanut Mixture

3 cups (750 ml) water
2 lbs (900 g) stew beef, cubed
$2^1/2$ cups (625 ml) coconut cream
2 potatoes, peeled and cubed
1 cup (200 g) roasted peanuts
$1/3$ cup (100 ml) fish sauce
$1/3$ cup (70 g) Thai palm sugar
$1/3$ cup (100 ml) Tamarind Juice (page 20)

Preparation time: 10 MINUTES, PLUS 20 MINUTES FOR SOAKING
Cooking time: 55 TO 60 MINUTES
Makes 6 TO 8 SERVINGS

1 Place all curry paste ingredients, except the water and the salt, in a dry skillet over medium heat. Roast, stirring, until brown and fragrant, for 5 to 7 minutes. Blend the roasted curry paste ingredients in a blender with the $1/2$ cup (125 ml) water until smooth; add extra water if the paste is too thick. Add the salt and set aside.

2 Pour the 3 cups (750 ml) water into a large stockpot and bring to a boil over medium heat. Add the beef and simmer until tender, about 40 minutes. Remove from the heat.

3 Bring the coconut cream to a boil over medium heat in a wok or large saucepan. Add the curry paste and cook, stirring regularly to prevent burning, until it becomes fragrant, about 5 minutes.

4 Stir this mixture in with the simmered meat. Add the potatoes and the peanuts. Reduce the heat to low and cook for another 15 to 20 minutes, or until the potatoes are fork-tender. Add the fish sauce, palm sugar, and tamarind juice. Stir until the sugar is dissolved. Serve hot.

Red Curry with Pork and Eggplant

Kang Phet Muu

Kang phet means "spicy curry" in Thailand, but in America this dish is usually called Red Curry. Whatever the translation, this dish is delicious and versatile. Beef, pork, fish, or shellfish may all be used in place of chicken. If you cannot find the small green round Thai eggplant, you may substitute bamboo shoots, cauliflower, or Asian eggplant.

Curry Paste
5 dried chilies, or to taste, soaked in cold water for 20 minutes
3 shallots, peeled and quartered
3 cloves garlic, peeled
Three 1/8-in (3-mm) thick slices galangal, shredded
1/2 cup (50 g) thinly sliced lemongrass
3 fresh coriander roots
1 tablespoon toasted coriander seeds
1 teaspoon toasted cumin seeds
1 teaspoon minced kaffir lime rind
1 teaspoon shrimp paste
1 teaspoon salt
10 whole black peppercorns
1/2 cup (125 ml) water, or more as needed

Eggplant & Pork Mixture
2 1/2 cups (625 ml) coconut cream
1 lb (500 g) pork, thinly sliced into bite-sized pieces
8 round Thai eggplants, quartered
20 fresh Thai basil leaves
3 kaffir lime leaves, torn into small pieces
2 tablespoons fish sauce
2 teaspoons palm sugar

Preparation time: 20 MINUTES, PLUS 20 MINUTES FOR SOAKING
Cooking time: 20 MINUTES
Makes 4 TO 6 SERVINGS

1 Combine all curry paste ingredients in a blender. Purée until smooth, adding more water as needed. Set aside.

2 Scoop out 1 1/2 cups (325 ml) of coconut cream into a saucepan and bring it to a boil over medium heat, stirring occasionally. Add the curry paste and cook for about 5 minutes, or until the mixture becomes fragrant. Stir in the remaining 1 cup (250 ml) coconut cream. Add the meat and bring the mixture to a boil again. Reduce the heat to low and cook until the meat is tender. Add the vegetables and cook until they are soft, about 5 more minutes. Add the Thai basil leaves, kaffir lime leaves, fish sauce, and sugar. Stir until the sugar is dissolved. Serve hot.

Chapter 6

Thai Noodles and Rice Dishes

Noodles and rice are equally popular In Thailand. At dinner, however, it's usually rice that is served; noodles are almost exclusively a lunchtime food. Says Nongkran Daks, "Office people eat noodles, which are available on every corner in big cities. The people who eat rice for lunch are laborers and taxi drivers. This is because a bowl of noodles costs as much as a full plate of rice with curry. And the noodles come in fairly small portions, whereas one serving of rice and curry makes quite a filling meal."

In the south, people usually eat curry over rice for lunch. Rural Thais in the north and northeast often have sticky rice with grilled meat. They even eat this for breakfast, perhaps with a dish like Green Papaya Salad (page 66) alongside.

Chiang Mai Noodles with Beef Curry Sauce *Khao Soi Nua*

This curry originated in Burma and was adapted to local Thai ingredients and tastes. Known as *Kaukswe* in Burma, it is popular in Northern Thailand as a lunch staple. This one-pot curry can be made ahead of time—the flavors actually intensify by the second day—and makes a great winter meal. It also freezes well. If you serve this as part of a full Thai meal rather than a standalone dish, reduce the amount of coconut milk to 2 cups. And be sure to offer each person a pair of chopsticks plus a soup spoon. Pickled mustard greens can be found in Asian markets.

Preparation time: 15 MINUTES, PLUS 20 MINUTES
FOR SOAKING
Cooking time: 10 MINUTES
Makes 6 TO 8 SERVINGS

Curry Paste

7 dried chilies, soaked in cold
    water for 20 minutes
12 cloves garlic, peeled and
    chopped
Ten $1/8$-in (3-mm) thick slices
    fresh ginger
5 cardamom pods, inner seeds
    only
5 whole cloves
1 small yellow onion, peeled
    and coarsely chopped
$1/2$ whole nutmeg kernel
1 tablespoon plus 1 teaspoon
    curry powder
1 tablespoon coriander seeds,
    toasted
1 teaspoon cumin seeds,
    toasted
1 teaspoon ground cinnamon
1 teaspoon shrimp paste
1 blade mace, or $1/2$ teaspoon
    ground mace
$1/2$ cup (125 ml) water, or more
    as needed

Beef & Noodle Mixture

Three $13^1/2$-oz (400-ml) cans
    coconut milk
4 tablespoons fish sauce
1 teaspoon salt
1 teaspoon sugar
2 lbs (900 g) beef, cut into 2
    x 1 x $1/8$-in (5-cm x 2.5-cm x
    3-mm) pieces
2 lbs (900 g) fresh egg
    noodles, $1/4$ lb (225 g) set
    aside for deep-frying
2 cups (500 ml) vegetable oil
    for frying
2 green onions (scallions),
    thinly sliced
1 lb (500 g) pickled mustard
    greens, cut crosswise into
    small pieces
2 stems fresh coriander,
    coarsely chopped
2 limes or lemons, cut in half
    lengthwise and then into
    thirds

1 Combine all curry paste ingredients in a blender. Purée until smooth, adding more water as needed. Set aside.

2 Heat 2 cups of the coconut milk in a large wok over medium heat. When the milk starts to boil, stir in the curry paste and cook, stirring, for about 5 minutes, or until fragrant. Add the fish sauce, salt, and sugar, stirring well after each addition.

3 Add the beef to the coconut milk mixture and stir well to mix. When the mixture comes to a boil again, add the remaining coconut milk. Stir well and remove from the heat.

4 Meanwhile, bring a large pot of water to a boil. Add 1¾ lbs (725 g) of the noodles. Cook until just soft, about 3 minutes. Drain and set aside.

5 Heat 2 cups of oil in a medium saucepan to 350 degrees. Drop one fresh noodle strand into the oil; if it turns golden, the oil is ready. Put the remaining ¼ lb (225 g) of noodles onto a plate and spread them out to avoid clumps. Fry half in the hot oil, turning once, until noodles are golden brown, 20 to 30 seconds. Remove from the oil and spread on paper towels to drain. Repeat with remaining noodles, and reserve as garnish.

6 To serve, scoop a portion of boiled noodles into each individual bowl and top with a ladle of curry. Garnish with crispy noodles, green onions, pickled mustard greens, and fresh coriander. Pass the lemon or lime sections.

Fresh Rice Noodles with Beef and Thai Basil *Kuay Tiaw Khee Mao Nua*

Commonly nicknamed "drunken noodles," this very popular noodle dish originated in Thailand. Authorities offer several explanations for the unusual name: it's a hangover food; the cook was drunk when he created it; or you must be drunk to enjoy the chili heat. Whatever the origin, this noodle dish has legions of fans at Thai restaurants worldwide.

Chicken, pork, or shrimp may be used instead of beef in this recipe. The Golden Mountain brand of soy sauce, which is a Thai product, has a slightly different flavor from typical salty soy sauce, even though it is made from soybeans, because it contains a small amount of sugar.

Preparation time: 5 MINUTES
Cooking time: 5 MINUTES
Makes 2 SERVINGS

Seasoning Sauce
1 tablespoon fish sauce
1 tablespoon soy sauce, preferably Golden Mountain brand
1 tablespoon oyster sauce
1 tablespoon sweet dark soy sauce

Noodle Mixture
3 tablespoons vegetable oil
2 cloves garlic, peeled and finely chopped
1/2 lb (250 g) thinly sliced beef
1/2 small yellow onion, peeled and cut lengthwise into 5 wedges
12 oz (375 g) fresh rice noodles, separated (see page 17)
1 cup (225 g) cut Chinese or Western broccoli
1 cup (30 g) Thai basil leaves
1 red chili, sliced or chopped

1 Combine all seasoning sauce ingredients in a small bowl. Whisk to blend and set aside.

2 Heat the 3 tablespoons of the oil in a large wok over medium heat and stir-fry the garlic until golden, about 3 minutes. Add the beef and the onion and stir-fry for 2 to 3 minutes more, until the beef no longer looks rare. Add the noodles and seasoning sauce, and stir several times. Add the Chinese broccoli, basil leaves, and chili, stirring well to combine after each addition. Serve immediately.

Old-Fashioned Fried Rice with Thai Basil and Crispy Shallots *Khao Pat Horapa*

Thais love to enjoy this simple, fast lunch dish with a bowl of *Tom Yum* soup (page 50). There are three kinds of basil in Thailand: lemon basil, Thai basil, and holy basil. Though holy basil is traditionally used for this dish, it is hard to find in the West. Thai basil is a good substitute.

Preparation time: 5 MINUTES
Cooking time: ABOUT 10 MINUTES
Makes 2 SERVINGS

4 tablespoons vegetable oil
3 cloves garlic, peeled and finely chopped
1 red or green chili, minced, or more to taste (optional)
1 cup (200 g) thinly sliced chicken breast
4 cups (700 g) cooked jasmine rice
2 tablespoons fish sauce
1 tablespoon soy sauce
20 Thai basil leaves
2 tablespoons Crispy Shallots (page 26)
1 cucumber, thinly sliced
1 lime, cut into quarters

1 Heat the oil in a large wok over medium heat. Add the garlic and minced chili, if using. Stir-fry until the garlic turns golden, about 3 minutes. Add the chicken and stir-fry for 2 to 3 minutes. Add the rice and continue to cook, stirring often, for 2 to 3 minutes more. Add the fish sauce, soy sauce, and basil leaves, and stir well to combine.

2 Spoon the mixture onto a serving platter and garnish with fresh basil and crispy shallots. Serve with cucumber slices and several squeezes of fresh lime juice, if desired.

Noodles with Fish Curry Sauce

Khanom Jeen Nam Ya

Khanom jeen, meaning "Chinese round rice noodles," refers to a type of noodle from southern China. *Nam ya,* which means "medicinal soup" in Thai, indicates that many herbs and spices are used in this recipe. This old-fashioned dish is usually served at ceremonies or at big gatherings, such as New Year's celebrations, birthday parties, or weddings. Note that lemon basil is usually only available at Asian markets during the summer months; Thai basil, which is available all year, may be used instead. Guilin rice vermicelli is a rather unusual type of noodle, but it can be found in Asian markets, as can pickled mustard greens.

Fish & Noodle Mixture
4 cups (1 liter) water
2 lbs (900 g) whole fish, such as rockfish, sea bass or red snapper, or 1 lb (500 g) fish fillets
4 cups (1 liter) coconut milk
1/4 cup (60 ml) fish sauce
2 lbs (900 g) Guilin rice vermicelli, cooked according to package directions (15 min), drained and rinsed under cold water

Curry Paste
7 dried chilies, soaked in cold water for 20 minutes
4 oz (135 g) rhizome (see sidebar)
6 cloves garlic, peeled and chopped
4 shallots, peeled and quartered
Six 1/8-in (3-mm) thick slices galangal, shredded
1/4 cup (60 g) chopped lemongrass
1 tablespoon shrimp paste
1 teaspoon kaffir lime zest

Accompaniments
1 cup (120 g) mung bean sprouts, blanched
1 cup (230 g) lemon or Thai basil leaves
1 cup (130 g) cut-up pickled mustard greens
6 hard-boiled eggs, peeled and sliced in half

Preparation Time: 30 MINUTES, PLUS 20 MINUTES FOR SOAKING AND 15 MINUTES FOR COOKING NOODLES
Cooking Time: 30 MINUTES
Makes 12 SERVINGS

1 Bring the water to a boil in a large saucepan over medium heat. Add the fish and simmer for about 10 minutes. Remove the fish, reserving the stock for later use. Bone the fish if not using fillets. Pound the fish meat with a mortar and pestle or grind it in a blender with some fish stock until fluffy. Set aside.

2 Combine all curry paste ingredients in a blender with 1 cup of the reserved fish stock. Purée until smooth and set aside.

3 Bring the coconut milk to a boil in a large saucepan over medium heat and allow to boil for 3 to 4 minutes. Add the curry paste, stirring well. Cook for 3 to 4 minutes more. Add the fish meat and fish sauce to the saucepan, stirring to prevent the fish from clumping. Cook for 5 minutes more, or until the sauce has thickened. Remove from the heat.

4 To serve, arrange the accompaniments on a serving platter. Scoop 1 cup noodles into a bowl and top with some accompaniments. Spoon some fish mixture over the noodles. Repeat until each person is served.

Rhizome

Generically speaking, a rhizome is a plant stem that grows horizontally underground and sends up shoots. But in Southeast Asian cuisine, "rhizome" refers to a member of the ginger family also known as "lesser galangal," a specific cluster of fingerlike roots with a distinctive flavor and aroma. Rhizome is used in seafood dishes, curries, and assorted stir-fries not only in Thailand, but throughout Southeast Asia. It is not likely to be found in a Western market, but it is sometimes available fresh, and can usually be found in the freezer case, in Asian markets. It also comes in pickled form. Powdered rhizome may be found in Asian markets, but it is not recommended, as the unique gingery flavor may be lost.

Pad Thai *Kuay Tiaw Pad Thai*

This popular dish takes time to prepare. However, you can make the sauce in advance and keep it in the freezer or refrigerator. For an authentic dish, don't take shortcuts, and don't leave out any of the ingredients—particularly in the Pad Thai sauce, which gives the final dish its rich amber color and succulent taste. Preserved or salted radish is sold in cellophane packets at Asian markets; it lasts almost indefinitely in the refrigerator. Select the rice stick noodles marked "M" for medium; other widths are used for other noodle dishes. If you want to double this recipe, do not double the ingredients. Instead, make the dish twice. If you plan to make Pad Thai for company, cook the noodles ahead of time and add the bean sprouts and garlic chives when you heat it up. If it is an informal gathering, your guests may enjoy assembling their own Pad Thai. Be sure to have all ingredients within easy reach: you have to work fast and be at the stove throughout the cooking time. It is worth the effort, however—with one bite of this Pad Thai, you will discover noodle heaven—and understand how it won the Throwdown challenge with Bobby Flay.

Preparation Time: 60 MINUTES, PLUS 60 MINUTES FOR SOAKING
Cooking Time: 5 MINUTES
Makes 2 SERVINGS

Shrimp & Noodle Mixture

4 tablespoons vegetable oil, or more as needed
1 teaspoon chopped garlic
1 tablespoon dried shrimp (optional)
1/2 cup (165 g) sliced cooked pork (optional)
1/2 cup (165 g) whole shrimp, shelled and deveined
1 tablespoon shredded preserved radish
1/4 lb (125 g) medium-size dried rice noodles, soaked 60 minutes in cold water and drained
5 to 6 tablespoons Pad Thai Sauce (recipe follows)
2 large eggs
1/2 teaspoon ground dried hot chilies, or more to taste
2 tablespoons ground roasted peanuts
1/2 cup (100 g) sliced garlic chives or green onions (scallions)
2 cups (220 g) bean sprouts, rinsed, plus more for garnish
2 wedges lime

Pad Thai Sauce

1 cup (250 ml) Tamarind Juice (page 20)
1 cup (200 g) palm sugar
1 cup (250 ml) water
1/2 cup (125 ml) fish sauce
2 teaspoons salt

 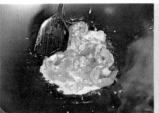 

Frying Pad Thai

1 Assemble all the ingredients.

2 Stir-fry the egg and shrimp in a wok for about 2 minutes, or until the shrimp turns pink. Alternatively, you can add the egg towards the end of cooking as the instructions note below.

3 Add the remaining ingredients and stir-fry quickly to combine. Add the chilies, peanuts, garlic chives, and bean sprouts last. Stir to combine before serving.

1 Prepare the Pad Thai sauce. You can buy premixed tamarind concentrate or make your own Tamarind Juice, see page 20. This sauce keeps well in the refrigerator for several months. Be sure to cool the sauce before use. It adheres better to the noodles when cold, so they will absorb the flavors more fully.

2 Combine all sauce ingredients in a saucepan and cook over medium-low heat for about 60 minutes, until syrupy. Stir occasionally to prevent burning. Allow to cool.

3 Heat the oil in a wok. Add the garlic and stir-fry until golden brown. Add the shrimp and pork, if using, and keep stirring until the shrimp changes color. Remove the shrimp to prevent overcooking and set aside. Stir in the dried shrimp, if using, and preserved radish.

4 Add the noodles. They will stick together, so stir fast and try to keep them separate. Add a little water, stirring a few times. Add the Pad Thai sauce and continue stirring until all ingredients are thoroughly mixed. The noodles should appear soft and moist. Return the cooked shrimp to the wok.

5 Push the contents of the wok up around the sides to make room to fry the eggs. If the pan is very dry, add 1 more tablespoon of oil. Add the eggs, stir lightly to break yolks, and cover them with the noodles. When the eggs are cooked, stir them into the noodles until everything is well mixed; this should result in cooked bits of eggs, both whites and yolk, throughout the noodle mixture.

6 Add the chilies, peanuts, garlic chives, and bean sprouts. Mix well. Transfer to a serving platter. Serve with raw bean sprouts, lime wedges, and a few squeezes of lime juice.

Noodles with Shrimp and Mung Bean Sauce *Khanom Jeen Nam Prik*

Jeen Nam Prik and *Khanom Jeen Nam Ya* (page 112) are usually offered to-gether: both are old-fashioned Thai dishes and are served at special gather-ings. This particular recipe contains some unusual ingredients, all of which should be available at Asian markets. Water convolvulus, also known as "water spinach" in English and *ong choi* in Chinese, is a leafy green vegetable. Mung beans are small green beans that sprout easily when left in water for several hours or overnight. Look for the kaffir lime, most likely frozen, in Asian or Thai markets. If kaffir limes are unavailable, Western limes may be substituted in this case. Guilin rice vermicelli is an unusual type of noodle, but it is also sold at Asian markets.

Banana blossoms or flowers grow in clusters at the ends of immature bananas and are sheathed in a purplish outer husk. Once the husk is peeled away, the blossoms inside are as edible as bananas. Sometime available fresh at Asian markets, but also sold canned, banana blossoms can be added to a variety of dishes. To prepare, remove the outer husk, then cut the flower in half lengthwise. Rub briefly with lime juice and shred thinly crosswise. Immediately soak the shredded blossoms in tamarind water until ready to use to prevent discoloring.

Preparation Time: 30 MINUTES, PLUS 8 HOURS AND 20 MINUTES FOR SOAKING
Cooking Time: 30 MINUTES
Makes 8 SERVINGS

Shrimp & Noodle Mixture
1 cup (200 g) peeled mung beans, soaked overnight and drained
4 cups (1 liter) coconut milk
1 cup (200 g) finely chopped shrimp meat
1/2 cup (115 g) Thai Chili Paste (*nam prik pao*, page 22)
3 kaffir lime leaves, torn into small pieces
1/4 cup (60 ml) fish sauce
1/4 cup (60 ml) fresh lime juice
1/4 cup (60 ml) Tamarind Juice (page 20)
3/4 cup (150 g) palm sugar
1/2 cup (50 g) chopped fresh coriander
1 kaffir lime, cut in half crosswise
1/2 cup (100 g) Crispy Shallots (page 26)
2 lbs (900 g) Guilin rice vermicelli, cooked according to package instructions (15 min), drained and rinsed under cold water

Curry Paste
5 dried red chilies, soaked in water for 20 minutes
5 shallots, peeled and quartered
5 cloves garlic, peeled and chopped
Three 1/8-in (3-mm) thick slices galangal, shredded
1/2 cup (125 ml) water

Accompaniments
1 cup (150 g) shredded banana blossoms
6 hard-boiled eggs, peeled and quartered
1 cup (130 g) chopped, blanched water convolvulus

1 Steam the soaked and drained mung beans in a steamer over high heat for 30 minutes. Allow to cool, then grind to a paste in a food processor or blender to make 2 cups of bean paste. Set aside 1 cup for use in this recipe; freeze the remainder in a tightly sealed container for future use.

2 Combine all curry paste ingredients in a blender. Purée until smooth, adding more water as needed. Set aside.

3 Heat the coconut milk over medium heat in a large saucepan until boiling. Add the curry paste, stirring well, and cook for 4 to 5 minutes. Add the shrimp meat and the chili paste, stirring constantly to prevent the shrimp from clumping. Add the kaffir lime leaves.

4 Reduce the heat to low. Add the fish sauce, lime juice, tamarind juice, and palm sugar. Stir in the chopped fresh coriander, kaffir lime, and crispy shallots. Remove from the heat.

5 To serve, arrange the accompaniments on a platter. Scoop 1 cup noodles into a bowl and top with some accompaniments. Spoon the shrimp mixture over everything. Repeat until each person is served.

Fresh Rice Noodles with Chinese Broccoli and Pork Kuay Tiaw Pat Si Ew Muu

This noodle dish is my husband's favorite. Although it is presumably Chinese in origin, I never found it during the four years we lived in Beijing. Look for fresh wide rice noodles, which are known as *sen yai* in Thailand, in an Asian market. Chinese broccoli, or *pak khana*, is a commonly used green vegetable in many Asian countries, so it should be readily available in Asian markets in the West. I suggest using a nonstick skillet to cut down on amount of oil needed and to keep the noodles from sticking together.

Preparation Time: 15 MINUTES
Cooking Time: 5 MINUTES
Makes 2 SERVINGS

Seasoning Sauce
1 tablespoon fish sauce
1 tablespoon oyster sauce
1 tablespoon granulated sugar
1 tablespoon soy sauce
1 tablespoon dark sweet soy sauce

Chili Vinegar For Sprinkling
1/4 cup (75 ml) apple cider vinegar
2 fresh green or red chilies, thinly sliced
   crosswise

Noodle Mixture
1/2 lb (250 g) Chinese broccoli
3 to 4 tablespoons vegetable oil
3 cloves garlic, peeled and finely
   chopped
1/2 lb (250 g) boneless pork, thinly sliced
12 oz (375 g) fresh wide rice noodles
2 large eggs

1 Combine all seasoning sauce ingredients. Whisk to blend and set aside. Combine the cider vinegar and chili slices in a small bowl and set aside.
2 Peel the tough stems of the Chinese broccoli and discard. Cut into 2-inch (5-cm) lengths. Rinse under cold water and set aside.

3 Heat 3 tablespoons of the vegetable oil in a large wok over medium heat. Fry the garlic until golden brown. Add the pork and stir a few times until the meat changes color. Add the noodles and seasoning sauce and stir a few times.
4 Push the noodles up around the sides of the wok. If the wok is very dry, add 1 more tablespoon vegetable oil. Add the eggs and cover them with the noodles. Allow eggs to cook, about 2 minutes, then stir into the noodles until everything is well mixed. Add the broccoli and stir to combine. Transfer to a serving platter. Sprinkle the mixture with the chili vinegar to taste before serving.

Chicken with Snow Peas and Bamboo Shoots Over Rice *Khao Na Kai*

Thais are very fond of this one-dish luncheon meal. For those who are vegetarian, the chicken may be left out and extra mushrooms and bean curd used in its place, and the chicken stock can be replaced with vegetable stock. Soy sauce may be substituted for the fish sauce and oyster sauce if desired.

Preparation Time: 5 MINUTES, PLUS 1 HOUR FOR MARINATING
Cooking Time: 7 MINUTES
Makes 2 SERVINGS

Seasoning Sauce
1 cup (250 ml) chicken stock
1 tablespoon oyster sauce
1 tablespoon fish sauce

Chicken Mixture
1/2 lb (250 g) thinly sliced boneless, skinless chicken breast
2 tablespoons soy sauce
1 tablespoon sesame oil
2 tablespoons tapioca flour
3 tablespoons vegetable oil
2 cloves garlic, peeled and finely chopped
1 cup (100 g) sliced fresh mushrooms
1/2 cup (50 g) sliced bamboo shoots
12 snow peas, ends trimmed
1/4 teaspoon freshly ground black pepper
4 cups (700 g) cooked jasmine rice
1 stem fresh coriander, coarsely chopped (optional, for garnish)

1 Combine all seasoning sauce ingredients in a small bowl and set aside.

2 Place the chicken pieces in a large bowl. Add the soy sauce, sesame oil, and tapioca flour. Mix together gently by hand. Allow the chicken to marinate for about 1 hour.

3 Heat the vegetable oil in a wok over medium heat. Add the garlic and stir-fry until golden, about 3 minutes. Add the chicken and stir-fry for about 1 minute, or until the meat turns white. Stir in the mushrooms, bamboo shoots, and snow peas. Pour in the seasoning sauce and continue cooking, stirring constantly, until the sauce thickens and becomes clear. Add the black pepper and adjust seasonings to taste.

4 Arrange the cooked rice on a platter and spoon the chicken mixture over top. Garnish with the fresh coriander, if desired.

Fried Rice with Pineapple, Ham, and Raisins *Khao Pad Saparot*

Any meat may be used in this recipe, but fresh—not canned—pineapple makes all the difference. As shown in the photo below, feel free to add tomato, green peas, and corn for extra color and nutrition. Prepared crispy shallots are available in Asian markets, but you can also make them yourself (page 26). As for the ham, cut lunchmeat-size slices into pieces.

Preparation time: 5 MINUTES
Cooking time: 5 MINUTES
Makes 2 SERVINGS

Seasoning Sauce
1 tablespoon oyster sauce
1 tablespoon fish sauce
1 tablespoon light soy sauce or Golden Mountain brand soy sauce
1 teaspoon granulated sugar
½ teaspoon freshly ground white pepper

Fried Rice
2 tablespoons vegetable oil
3 cloves garlic, peeled and finely chopped
1 cup (120 g) chopped cooked ham
½ small onion, peeled and diced
2 eggs, lightly beaten
4 cups (700 g) cooked jasmine rice
½ cup (200 g) diced fresh pineapple
1 green onion (scallion), thinly sliced
2 tablespoons raisins
1 fresh red chili, cut into slivers
1 cucumber, thinly sliced

1 Combine all seasoning sauce ingredients in a small bowl. Whisk to blend and set aside.

2 Heat the oil in a wok over medium heat. Add the garlic and stir-fry until golden, about 3 minutes. Add the ham and the onion and stir a few times. Add the eggs, stirring quickly so they won't set. Stir in the rice, mixing well, and continue to cook until the contents are thoroughly heated. Add the pineapple, the seasoning sauce, the green onion, and the raisins, stirring well to combine after each addition.

3 Transfer to a serving platter. Garnish with the chili slivers. Serve with sliced cucumber alongside.

Shrimp and Crabmeat Fried Rice

Khao Pat Puu, Kung

Given Thailand's long coastline, it comes as no surprise that locally caught shrimp and crab are delicious. Fried rice is originally Chinese, but this Thai version is lighter and more delicate than the Chinese version. This dish is a favorite among urban workers on the go in Thailand. However, with the global demand for Thai seafood skyrocketing, this simple dish can no longer be considered an inexpensive street food.

Preparation time: 5 MINUTES
Cooking time: 5 MINUTES
Makes 2 SERVINGS

Seasoning Sauce
1 tablespoon oyster sauce
1 tablespoon fish sauce
1 tablespoon soy sauce
$\frac{1}{2}$ teaspoon granulated sugar (optional)
$\frac{1}{2}$ teaspoon freshly ground white pepper

Fried Rice
3 tablespoons vegetable oil
2 cloves garlic, peeled and finely chopped
6 fresh large shrimp, peeled and deveined
$\frac{1}{2}$ small onion, peeled and cut lengthwise into 8 wedges
$\frac{1}{2}$ small tomato, cut lengthwise into 4 wedges
2 eggs, lightly beaten
4 cups (700 g) cooked jasmine rice
1 cup (450 g) lump crabmeat, picked clean
2 lime wedges
1 cucumber, thinly sliced crosswise

1 Combine all seasoning sauce ingredients in a small bowl. Whisk to blend and set aside.

2 Heat the oil in a wok over medium heat. Add the garlic and stir-fry until golden, about 3 minutes. Add the shrimp, onion, and tomato, and stir a few times. Add the eggs, stirring quickly so they won't set. Stir in the rice and seasoning sauce, mixing well, and continue to cook until the contents are heated through. Stir in the crabmeat.

3 Transfer to a serving platter. Garnish with the sliced cucumber and lime wedges.

Chicken Rice _Khao Man Kai_

This dish, the Thai version of what was originally a specialty of the Chinese island of Hainan, is a popular street lunch food throughout Thailand. Unlike its Chinese cousin, this version is accompanied by a salty-pungent sauce made from fermented soybeans, making it distinctly Thai. Both yellow bean sauce and red vinegar, or Chinese red vinegar, which is composed of red rice and barley, are available in Asian markets and from online Asian grocers. Ideally, the meat should be from an organically raised capon (castrated rooster). However, any plump roasting chicken will do. A few Thai-Chinese and Hainanese descendants still use capons raised in Nakorn Pathom, not far from Bangkok. In the United States, capons are considered a delicacy, and may be ordered from specialty markets and online sources. The pandan leaves are optional, but they really enhance the flavor of the rice soup. In Thailand, this rice dish is often served alongside Winter Melon Soup, page 53.

Preparation time: 15 MINUTES
Cooking time: 60 MINUTES
Makes 8 TO 10 SERVINGS

Bean Sauce

2 tablespoons yellow bean
  sauce
4 cloves garlic, peeled and
  chopped
Three 1/8-in (3-mm) thick slices
  fresh ginger
1/4 cup (65 ml) red vinegar or
  red wine vinegar
3 tablespoons soy sauce
2 tablespoons chicken stock
1 teaspoon granulated sugar

Capon with Rice

One 5-lb (2-kg) capon or
  roasting chicken, rinsed and
  dried
1 tablespoon salt
Two 1-in (2.5-cm) long pieces
  fresh ginger, peeled and
  crushed
10 cups (2.5 liters) water
Vegetable oil, if needed
6 cloves garlic, peeled and
  finely chopped
4 cups (700 g) uncooked long-
  grain rice
7 cups (1.75 liters) chicken stock
3 pandan leaves, tied in a knot
  (optional)
2 cucumbers, peeled and thinly
  sliced
3 stems fresh coriander,
  coarsely chopped

1 Combine all bean sauce ingredients in a blender and process until smooth. This should make about 1 cup of sauce.

2 Remove the extra fat from the chicken and render it over low heat in a large saucepan suitable for cooking rice. Rub the salt over the chicken, inside and out. Place one piece of the crushed ginger in the body cavity.

3 Bring the water to a boil in a Dutch oven over high heat. Add the capon, cover, reduce the heat to medium, and cook for 30 minutes. Turn the bird over and cook, covered, for 30 minutes more. Take the Dutch oven off the heat, but leave the chicken in the pot until you begin to cook the rice, 30 to 45 minutes before serving time.

4 When you are ready to cook the rice, remove the thoroghly cooked capon from the Dutch oven and let it cool to room temperature. When it is cool enough to handle, bone the meat and chop it into bite-sized pieces. Set aside.

5 There should be about 1/2 cup rendered chicken fat in the second saucepan. If necessary, add vegetable oil to make up this amount. Heat the fat over medium heat. Sauté the garlic until lightly browned. Add the rice, stirring to coat the rice grains with fat. Add the chicken stock, pandan leaves (if using), and the second piece of ginger. Bring this mixture to a boil over high heat and cook until nearly all the liquid is absorbed. Reduce the heat to low, cover, and cook for about 20 minutes without stirring. Remove from the heat and spoon the rice onto a serving platter.

6 Place the capon meat attractively on the rice. Garnish with cucumber slices around the edge of the platter and fresh coriander leaves in the center. Pass with the bean sauce.

American Fried Rice *Khao Pad American*

One of the most interesting dishes created in Thailand is one that, despite its name, is rarely found in the US. What Thais call "American Fried Rice" was created by Thai cooks during the Vietnam War era to give American servicemen stationed in or visiting Thailand something resembling their idea of American cooking. *Khao Pad* American has become very popular, especially among children. Use deli ham sold as lunchmeat; it is the correct size.

Preparation Time: 5 MINUTES
Cooking Time: 7 MINUTES
Makes 2 SERVINGS

2 cups (300 g) cooked jasmine rice
1 tablespoon light soy sauce
2 tablespoons ketchup
1/2 teaspoon salt
1/4 cup (60 ml) vegetable oil
2 large eggs
2 hot dogs
2 small slices ham
2 tablespoons butter
1/2 small yellow onion, peeled and diced
2 tablespoons raisins
1/4 cup (50 g) green peas
1/4 teaspoon ground black pepper

1 Combine the cooked rice with the soy sauce, ketchup, and salt in a mixing bowl. Set aside.

2 Heat the oil in a large skillet over medium heat and cook the eggs sunny-side up. When cooked, remove them from the skillet and set aside. Spiral-cut each hot dog, leaving the skin intact. In the same skillet, pan-fry the hot dogs and the ham until just golden. Remove from the skillet and set aside.

3 Melt the butter in the skillet and add the onion. Stir-fry until the onion is wilted, about 4 minutes. Add the rice, stirring until it is heated through. Stir in the raisins, green peas, and ground pepper. Mix to combine.

4 Scoop the rice onto a platter and arrange the hot dogs, eggs, and ham around it to serve.

Drunken Spaghetti with Shrimp

Spaghetti Khii Mao

Here's a great example of East meets West. Starting in the 1960s, American soldiers began arriving in large numbers in Thailand. To please the homesick soldiers, Thai cooks made an "American" version of Drunken Noodles, a traditional Thai dish, with spaghetti instead of rice noodles. While some may quibble about its authenticity, this dish is certainly easy to find in the growing number of upscale shopping malls throughout Bangkok and other major Thai cities.

Preparation Time: 5 MINUTES
Cooking Time: 15 MINUTES
Makes 4 SERVINGS

Seasoning Sauce

1 cup (250 ml) chicken stock
  or water
3 tablespoons soy sauce
3 tablespoons fish sauce
2 tablespoons sweet soy sauce
2 tablespoons white vinegar
1 teaspoon granulated sugar
  (optional)

Spaghetti & Shrimp

3 tablespoons vegetable oil
4 cloves garlic, peeled and
  chopped
1 lb (500 g) shrimp, shelled
  and deveined
5 cups (675 g) cooked
  spaghetti
8 cherry tomatoes, halved
1 cup (30 g) Thai basil or holy
  basil leaves
4 fresh Thai chilies, seeded and
  chopped

1 Combine all seasoning sauce ingredients in a small bowl. Whisk to blend, then set aside.

2 Heat the oil in a wok over medium heat. Add the garlic and stir-fry until golden, about 3 minutes. Add the shrimp and stir-fry until cooked through, about 3 minutes. Stir in the seasoning sauce. Add the cooked spaghetti and stir to combine well. Add the tomatoes, basil leaves and chilies. Stir again until well mixed and cook until heated through. Serve hot.

Stir-Fried Clams with Chili Paste and Thai Basil over Spaghetti

Hoi Pat Nam Prik Pao

There are many kinds of clams in Thailand. Thai cooks usually use cockles for this recipe. Unfortunately, the only cockles I've seen in the US are the frozen and imported ones that can be found in Asian grocery stories. Hard-shell clams work fine in this recipe, however. This dish becomes an interesting fusion with the addition of spaghetti as the base for the clams.

Preparation time: 5 MINUTES
Cooking time: 15 MINUTES
Makes 2 SERVINGS

3 tablespoons vegetable oil
4 cloves garlic, peeled and coarsely chopped
1 shallot, coarsely chopped
4 tablespoons Thai Chili Paste (*nam prik pao*, page 22)
1/2 cup (125 ml) chicken stock
2 lbs (900 g) small, hard-shell clams in their shells, scrubbed well
2 tablespoons fish sauce
1 cup (30 g) Thai basil leaves
2 fresh red chilies, seeded and sliced lengthwise (optional)
3 cups (450 g) cooked spaghetti

1 Heat the oil in a wok over medium heat. Add the garlic and shallot and stir-fry until the mixture turns golden, about 3 minutes. Stir in the chili paste and chicken stock until the mixture is smooth. Add the clams, cover, and cook until they open slightly, about 2 to 3 minutes.

2 Add the fish sauce, Thai basil, and chilies, and stir well. Increase the heat to medium-high and bring the mixture to a boil. Reduce the heat to medium and cook for 2 more minutes. To serve, place the cooked spaghetti on a serving platter and top with the clam mixture.

How to stir-fry clams
1 Assemble all the ingredients.
2 Stir-fry garlic, shallots, and Thai chili paste (*nam prik pao*) in a wok.
3 Add the clams.

Stir-Fried Noodles with Chicken and Thai Chili Paste *Ba Mee Nam Prik Pao*

Making this noodle dish is one way to use up any Thai chili paste left over after making *Tom Yum Kai* soup (page 50). If the chili paste is left out, this dish will taste very similar to Chinese lo mein, because it calls for fresh Chinese lo mein noodles. The Thai version is a little spicier and more flavorful.

Preparation time: 5 MINUTES
Cooking time: 15 MINUTES
Makes 2 SERVINGS

Seasoning Sauce

1/4 cup (60 ml) chicken stock or water
2 tablespoons Thai Chili Paste (*nam prik pao*, page 22)
2 tablespoons vinegar
1 tablespoon fish sauce
1 tablespoon soy sauce
1 tablespoon oyster sauce
1 teaspoon granulated sugar (optional)

Noodles & Chicken

1/2 lb (225 g) fresh egg noodles
3 tablespoons vegetable oil
2 cloves garlic, peeled and finely chopped
1/2 lb (225 g) chicken, cut into 2 x 1 x 1/3-in (5 x 2 x 1-cm) pieces
1 cup (60 g) fresh bean sprouts
1 cup (65 g) fresh snow peas
2 green onions (scallions), cut into 1-in (2.5-cm) pieces

1 Combine all seasoning sauce ingredients in a small bowl. Whisk to blend and set aside.
2 Bring a pot of water to a boil. Add the noodles and cook for 3 to 4 minutes; drain and rinse under cold water. Set aside.
3 Heat the vegetable oil in a wok over medium heat. Add the garlic and stir-fry until golden, about 3 minutes. Add the chicken and stir-fry until the meat turns white, 2 to 3 minutes. Add the noodles and seasoning sauce, stirring until well combined. Stir in the bean sprouts, snow peas, and green onions, and continue cooking until the ingredients are mixed well. Serve hot.

Chapter 7

Thai Vegetarian Dishes

Although many Thais participate in the annual vegetarian festival, and many Thai restaurants offer a vegetarian menu during this period, pure vegetarian food is not so easy to find: Thai curry pastes generally contain shrimp paste and fish sauce. But this is not an insurmountable barrier: tofu is ubiquitous. "It's actually easy to be vegetarian in Thailand," says Nongkran Daks, "because we make so much tofu. In the Chinatown market in Bangkok, you can find tofu that resembles duck, shrimp, or bacon. People like having these options so they don't feel so separate from their meat-eating friends and family. There are even sauces made for vegetarians, like vegetarian oyster sauce." Soft tofu is used in desserts and soup, and firmer varieties for stir-frying with noodle dishes or adding to curries. Soy milk is also readily available. Thai farmers now grow numerous varieties of fruits and vegetables, giving vegetarians even more dietary options.

Stir-Fried Bean Sprouts with Bean Curd and Snow Peas *Pat Tua Ngok Kap Tofu*

This is a good, economical side dish to serve with any curry. It also makes a substantial main dish for a vegetarian meal, and is very nutritious and simple to prepare. Be sure not to overcook the bean sprouts; they should still be crunchy.

Seasoning Sauce
3 tablespoons soy sauce, preferably Golden Mountain brand
1 teaspoon granulated sugar
1/2 teaspoon salt

Stir-Fried Bean Sprouts
3 tablespoons vegetable oil
3 garlic cloves, finely chopped
1/2 lb (225 g) bean curd, cut in half then sliced into 1/8-in (3-mm) thick pieces
2 to 3 tablespoons soy sauce
1 lb (500 g) fresh bean sprouts, cleaned
10 snow peas, strings removed and cut in half lengthwise
2 green onions (scallions), cut into 1-in (2.5-cm) long pieces

Preparation Time: 5 MINUTES
Cooking Time: 3 MINUTES
Makes 4 SERVINGS

1 Combine all the seasoning sauce ingredients in a small bowl. Whisk to blend and set aside.

2 Heat the oil in a wok over medium heat. Add the garlic and stir-fry until golden, about 3 minutes. Add the bean curd and lightly stir so that each piece is coated with oil. Sprinkle the soy sauce over the bean curd. Add the bean sprouts, snow peas, and seasoning sauce and stir until well combined. Stir in the green onions. Transfer to a platter and serve hot.

Stir-Fried Preserved Radish with Eggs and Green Onions *Pad Chai Poh Kap Khai*

Thais also enjoy this satisfying vegetarian dish at breakfast with soft-boiled rice—it's my grandson Noah's favorite. It also works well in a full Thai meal as a side dish for a curry or other spicy offering. Look for shredded preserved radish at any Asian market. Some cooks like to add Thai basil just before serving.

Preparation Time: 3 MINUTES
Cooking Time: 3 MINUTES
Makes 2 SERVINGS

2 tablespoons vegetable oil
3 garlic cloves, finely chopped
1/2 lb (225 g) shredded preserved radish
1 tablespoon palm sugar
2 large eggs
2 green onions (scallions), cut into 1-in
   (2.5-cm) long pieces
1 fresh red chili, slivered lengthwise
   (optional)

1 Heat the oil in a large wok over medium heat. Add the garlic and stir-fry until golden, about 3 minutes. Add the preserved radish and stir a few times. Add the palm sugar and stir until the sugar is dissolved.
2 Push the contents to the side of the wok. Crack the eggs into the center and cover with the radish mixture. Cook until the eggs are set. Add the green onions and slivered chili, if using. Stir to combine well and serve hot.

Stir-Fried Water Convolvulus with Soybean Sauce *Pad Pak Bung*

This well-loved Asian green has a number of different names: cooks also call it "water morning glory" and "water spinach" in English. In China, the Cantonese name is *ong choi*, and Thais call it *pak bung*. Note that this dish calls for high-temperature cooking (*fai dang*, literally "red fire"); it must be cooked fast so that the vegetables will still be green and crunchy. If you're eating out in Thailand and you find a dish called *pak bung fai dang*, you'll know what it is.

Preparation Time: 3 MINUTES
Cooking Time: ABOUT 6 MINUTES
Makes 4 SERVINGS

1 lb (500 g) water convolvulus, fresh
   spinach, or watercress
3 tablespoons vegetable oil
3 garlic cloves, finely chopped
3 fresh red Thai chilies, crushed (optional)
1 tablespoon yellow soybean sauce
2 tablespoons fish sauce
1/4 cup (60 ml) chicken stock

1 Wash the greens well and remove any tough stems or yellow leaves. Cut into 2-in (5-cm) lengths and set aside.

2 Heat the vegetable oil in a wok over high heat until very hot. Add the garlic; chilies, if using; and the soybean sauce. Stir-fry for about 3 minutes, or until the garlic turns golden. Add the greens, fish sauce, and chicken stock, stirring quickly until the ingredients are well combined, and the greens are tender but not overcooked. Serve immediately.

Bean Curd with Thai Basil

Tao Hu Pad Horapa

The beautiful aroma of Thai basil makes this simple dish one of my favorites! Nonvegetarians can add ½ lb (225 g) of any kind of meat. In addition, 1 tablespoon of fish sauce may be added to the seasoning sauce.

Preparation Time: 3 MINUTES
Cooking Time: ABOUT 6 MINUTES
Makes 2 SERVINGS

Seasoning Sauce

2 tablespoons soy sauce, preferably Golden Mountain brand
1 tablespoon light soy sauce
1 tablespoon sweet dark soy sauce
½ teaspoon salt

Bean Curd Mixture

3 tablespoons vegetable oil
2 cloves garlic, peeled and finely chopped
2 cups (200 g) thinly sliced fresh mushrooms
½ yellow onion, peeled, sliced in half and cut lengthwise into ½-in (12-mm) thick slices

2 green onions (scallions), cut into 1-in (2.5-cm) pieces
1 lb (500 g) bean curd, cut into 1-in (2.5-cm) squares
1 cup (30 g) fresh Thai basil leaves
3 red or green chilies, seeded and thinly sliced on the diagonal

1 Combine all seasoning sauce ingredients in a small bowl. Whisk to blend and set aside.
2 Heat the oil in a large wok over medium heat. Add the garlic and stir-fry until golden, about 3 minutes. Add the mushrooms, onion, and green onion, and stir-fry for about 1 minute. Add the bean curd and seasoning sauce, stirring well. Cook for about 2 minutes, then add the basil leaves and chilies. Mix well and serve.

Stir-Fried Asian Eggplant with Bean Curd and Thai Basil *Pad Makhua Yaaw Kap Tohu*

Simple and delicious, this entrée is a vegetarian delight. And you get the protein you need without the cholesterol! You will find long, slender Asian eggplants at well-stocked supermarkets and in Asian markets. Select those that are as straight as possible.

Preparation Time: 5 MINUTES
Cooking Time: 10 MINUTES
Makes 4 TO 6 SERVINGS

Seasoning Sauce
3/4 cup (190 ml) water
1 tablespoon soy sauce
1 tablespoon yellow bean sauce
1 teaspoon granulated sugar

Stir-Fried Eggplant
1/2 lb (250 g) bean curd, cut into 1-in (2.5-cm) cubes, drained on paper towels
Soy sauce for sprinkling
2 tablespoons vegetable oil
2 garlic cloves, peeled and finely chopped
2 cups (300 g) roll-cut Asian eggplant (see page 21)
2 green onions (scallions), cut into 1-in (2.5-cm) pieces
20 fresh Thai basil leaves
1 red chili, seeded and shredded lengthwise (optional)

Stir-frying Asian eggplant

1 Combine all seasoning sauce ingredients in a small bowl and mix. Set aside.
2 Place the bean curd cubes in a large bowl and sprinkle with a few drops of soy sauce. Set aside.
3 Heat the vegetable oil in a large wok over medium heat. Add the bean curd, being careful not to crowd the pieces. Fry until browned on all sides. Transfer to a bowl and set aside.

4 In the remaining oil in the wok, stir-fry the garlic until it turns golden, about 2 minutes. Add the eggplant and stir a few times. Add the seasoning sauce. Reduce the heat to medium-low, cover the wok, and cook about 5 minutes. Return the bean curd to the wok, stir a few times, and add the green onions, basil, and red chili, if using. Mix well and serve.

Vegetarian Curry with Bean Curd

Kang Phet Tofu

This curry certainly proves that a meal without meat can be both delicious and attractive. To save time, you can use commercial red curry paste in place of the recipe listed below. Other vegetables, such as cauliflower and mushrooms, can be substituted for some of those listed.

Preparation Time: 20 MINUTES, PLUS 20 MINUTES FOR SOAKING
Cooking Time: 20 MINUTES
Makes 4 TO 6 SERVINGS

Curry Paste

1/3 cup (100 ml) water, or more as needed
5 dried chilies, soaked in cold water for 20 minutes
3 shallots, peeled and quartered
3 garlic cloves, peeled and chopped
Three 1/2-in (12-mm) thick slices galangal, shredded
4 fresh coriander roots, coarsely chopped
1 teaspoon yellow bean sauce
1 teaspoon salt
1/2 teaspoon toasted coriander seeds
1/2 teaspoon toasted cumin seeds
1/2 teaspoon chopped kaffir lime rind
10 black peppercorns

Bean Curd Mixture

One 13.5-oz (400-ml) can coconut milk
4 cups (800 g) cut-up vegetables, such as green beans, baby corn, water chestnuts, bamboo shoots, eggplant and broccoli
1 1/2 lbs (750 g) bean curd, soft or hard, cut into 1/2-in (12-mm) squares
10 or more Thai basil leaves
3 kaffir lime leaves
2 tablespoons light soy sauce
1 teaspoon granulated sugar (optional)

1 Combine all curry paste ingredients in a blender. Purée until smooth, adding more water as needed. Set aside.

2 Pour the coconut milk into a saucepan and cook over medium heat until it bubbles. Stir in the curry paste and bring to a boil, cooking until the mixture becomes fragrant, about 5 minutes. Stir in the vegetables, mixing well. Add the bean curd, Thai basil leaves, kaffir lime leaves, and soy sauce. When the mixture comes to the boil again, stir in the sugar, if using, and cook for about 5 minutes more, or until heated through. Serve hot.

Tri-Color Pickles
Pak Dong Sam See

Years ago, I experimented with different combinations of pickled vegetables. Once, when I had a few extra broccoli stems, I came up with these colorful sweet and sour pickles. They make a tasty accompaniment to curry, and keep for months in a tightly sealed container in the refrigerator.

Preparation Time: 5 MINUTES
Marinating Time: 4 TO 6 HOURS
Makes 6 TO 8 SERVINGS

1 medium carrot, peeled
1 medium daikon radish, peeled
1 cucumber or 2 peeled broccoli stems
1 tablespoon salt
Ten 1/8-in (3-mm) thick slices ginger, shredded
2 fresh red chilies, seeded and sliced into 1/4-in (6-mm) rings (optional)
3/4 cup (100 ml) vinegar
3/4 cup (150 g) granulated sugar

1 Slice the carrot, daikon, and cucumber or broccoli stems crosswise into 1/4-in (6-mm) thick pieces to make about 4 cups sliced vegetables; alternatively, you can use the roll-cut method (page 21). Put the pieces into a non-reactive bowl and sprinkle with the salt, stirring to cover. Let stand for 4 to 6 hours.

2 Rinse the vegetables with cold water and dry with a paper towel. Put them in a glass jar. Add the ginger and chili slices, mixing well. Add the vinegar and sugar and stir to combine. Refrigerate for 5 days before eating.

Eggs with Tamarind Sauce Khai Look Khoey

Translated into English, the name of this dish, *Khai Look Khoey*, means "Son-in-Law Eggs." Tradition has it that a new son-in-law wanted to impress his wife's parents, so he invented this dish. They were so impressed that they named it after him! This side dish goes well with any curry.

Preparation time: 5 MINUTES
Cooking time: 10 MINUTES
Makes 6 SERVINGS

Seasoning Sauce
4 tablespoons Thai palm sugar
4 tablespoons Tamarind Juice (page 20)
3 tablespoons fish sauce or light soy sauce

Egg Mixture
2 tablespoons vegetable oil
6 hard-boiled eggs, shelled
3 tablespoons Crispy Shallots (page 26)
1 stem fresh coriander, coarsely chopped
1 red chili, slivered lengthwise

1 Combine all seasoning sauce ingredients in a saucepan. Cook over medium heat until slightly thickened, about 5 minutes. Set aside.

2 Heat the oil in a large skillet over medium heat. Add the whole hard-boiled eggs and carefully stir-fry them until golden brown. Remove from the skillet and allow to cool.

3 To serve, slice the eggs in half lengthwise and arrange on a serving platter. Pour the sauce over the eggs and garnish with the shallots, fresh coriander, and slivered chili.

Steamed Eggs *Khai Toon*

Small children and the elderly in particular love this egg dish. It is easy to digest and a snap to prepare. In the South, we use coconut milk in this dish, whereas elsewhere in Thailand chicken stock or water is used. I like to think of *Khai Toon* as my country's take on a soufflé. In the popular nonvegetarian version of *Khai Toon*, ground chicken or pork is included.

Preparation Time: 5 MINUTES
Cooking Time: 15 MINUTES
Makes 6 SERVINGS

4 extra-large eggs
1 cup (125 ml) water or coconut milk
3 tablespoons light soy sauce
1/2 teaspoon freshly ground white pepper
3 shallots, peeled and thinly sliced
2 green onions (scallions), including the
   green tops, finely chopped

1 Fill the bottom of a steamer with 2 inches (5 cm) of water and bring to a boil.
2 Crack the eggs into a bowl and beat lightly with a fork until smooth. Add all remaining ingredients. Stir to combine.
3 Divide the mixture into six 6-ounce (100-ml) custard cups, distributing evenly. Place the cups in the upper part of the steamer. Cover the steamer and steam the individual custards until the centers are set, about 7 minutes.

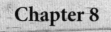

Chapter 8

Thai Desserts and Drinks

Even though some Thai sweets were introduced by foreigners, in Thailand they are not served after a large meal, like traditional Western desserts. Instead, they are eaten between meals as a snack, or in the early evenings after a light meal. After a big feast, Thais often have a piece of fruit. Ordering desserts in restaurants is relatively new. It is mainly done on weekends, by young couples out on a date or families eating together. Upscale restaurants do offer cakes and pies, as well as ice cream, fruit, or a few standard Thai desserts. However, the widest variety of Thai sweets is sold by pushcart vendors.

"In general, we cook desserts with all kinds of fruit, like Sweet Sticky Rice and Mangoes (page 148) or Pumpkin in Coconut Milk with Palm Sugar (page 146)," says Nongkran Daks. "We also use various types of bananas, tapioca, and young coconuts. In desserts like Sweet Black Rice Pudding (page 145) we even use sweet potatoes, taro, cassava, and other roots."

Iced coffee, tea, and limeade aren't desserts, but they're often enjoyed as mid-morning or afternoon sweet treats. Recently, due to pressure from Western chain coffee houses, as well as dietary concerns, traditional Thai drinks have undergone changes. Coffee is brewed without additional flavorings like roasted tamarind seeds, for example; and evaporated milk is used instead of sweetened condensed milk. These days, only beverages labeled "Ancient Coffee" or "Ancient Tea" might give you a chance to enjoy the same type of drinks Nongkran had while growing up.

Bananas and Tapioca in Sweet Coconut Milk Gluai Buad Chee

This dessert is fast and easy to make, and can be served hot or at room temperature. Loosely translated, *Gluai Buad Chee* means something like "Nun Banana," presumably because Buddhist nuns in Thailand wear white.

Preparation Time: 5 MINUTES
Cooking Time: 15 MINUTES
Makes 8 SERVINGS

6 ripe bananas, peeled and ends removed
4 tablespoons sesame seeds
2 cups (500 ml) water
One 13.5-oz (400 ml) can coconut milk
2/3 cup (160 g) granulated sugar
1/4 teaspoon salt (optional)
1/3 cup (65 g) small tapioca pearls, rinsed in cold water and drained

1 Slice bananas in half lengthwise. Cut each half into 4 slices to make a total of 48 pieces. Set aside.

2 Heat a dry skillet over medium heat. When hot, add the sesame seeds. Toast, stirring constantly, until brown, 2 to 3 minutes. Remove from the heat and set aside.

3 Combine the water, coconut milk, sugar, and salt, if using, in a 3-quart (3-liter) saucepan and bring to a boil. Reduce the heat to low and cook, stirring constantly, until the sugar dissolves. Add the tapioca and bananas. Continue cooking for 5 to 7 minutes more, stirring occasionally, until the tapioca pearls are clear and translucent.

4 Remove from the heat. Spoon into individual dessert bowls and sprinkle about ½ teaspoon toasted sesame seeds on top before serving.

Sweet Black Rice Pudding

Khao Niew Piak

Can you imagine eating rice as an entrée, then having rice for dessert? Thais certainly can! This black sticky rice dish, often enjoyed as an after-dinner treat, is a popular street vendor snack throughout Thailand. This is one of my most popular desserts, too. One of my customers had it after dinner and loved it so much he ordered an extra one for breakfast the next day. Look for black sticky rice (also called glutinous rice) at Asian supermarkets.

Preparation time: 5 MINUTES
Cooking time: 60 MINUTES
Makes 8 SERVINGS

1 cup (250 ml) black sticky rice, well rinsed
5 cups (1.25 liters) water
3 pandan leaves, tied into a knot
2 cups (400 g) taro, peeled and cut into 1/2-in (12-mm) cubes
1 cup (200 g) granulated sugar
1 cup (250 ml) coconut milk
1/2 teaspoon salt

1 Combine the rice and water in a large stockpot and bring to a boil. Add the pandan leaves, and reduce the heat to medium-low. Continue cooking for about 40 minutes, stirring occasionally.

2 Add the taro and continue to cook until soft, another 20 minutes. Remove from the heat, and discard the pandan leaves. Add the sugar and stir until it is dissolved.

3 Warm the coconut milk and salt in a small saucepan over low heat. To serve, spoon 3/4 cup rice pudding into a dessert bowl and top with 2 tablespoons coconut milk. May be eaten warm or at room temperature.

Pumpkin in Coconut Milk with Palm Sugar *Fak Thong Kang Buad*

Dense Japanese kabocha squash are similar in texture to Thai pumpkins, making them perfect for this dessert. You can find kabocha in Asian markets and some well-stocked supermarkets.

Preparation Time: 15 MINUTES
Cooking Time: 10 MINUTES
Makes 6 TO 8 SERVINGS

1 small kabocha squash (Japanese pumpkin), about 2 lbs (900 g)
2 cups (500 ml) coconut milk
1 cup (250 ml) water
½ cup (100 g) palm sugar
½ cup (100 g) granulated sugar
1 teaspoon salt

1 Wash the kabocha squash well and quarter it lengthwise. Scrape out the inner membrane and seeds, and pare off most of the skin; discard. Cut the flesh into uniform pieces about ½-inch (12-mm) thick.

2 In a medium saucepan, combine the remaining ingredients. Bring to a boil over medium heat and cook until the sugar is dissolved. Add the kabocha and continue cooking until tender but still firm, 7 to 10 minutes. Remove from the heat. Serve in small bowls, warm or at room temperature.

Tapioca Pudding with Shredded Young Coconut *Saku Mapraw On*

This unusual pudding is easy to make for a dessert or snack. It is usually available from street vendors, who will package it in a plastic bag so it can be enjoyed at home. Small tapioca pearls can be found in any Asian market. Do not try to substitute the instant tapioca sold in supermarkets. Tying the pandan leaves in a knot makes them easier to remove from the saucepan. Young coconut is available frozen in 1-pound (500-g) bags at an Asian market. Plan to use half the bag, including the liquid.

Preparation Time: 5 MINUTES
Cooking Time: 15 MINUTES
Makes 4 TO 6 SERVINGS

3 cups (750 ml) water
3 pandan leaves (optional), tied
   into a knot
1 cup (120 g) small tapioca pearls
1 cup (200 g) granulated sugar
1 cup (200 g) cooked, diced taro
   root or cooked corn kernels
   (optional)
1 cup (130 g) shredded young
   coconut, plus the juice
1 cup (250 ml) coconut milk
1/2 teaspoon salt
1 tablespoon tapioca starch or
   cornstarch mixed with
   2 tablespoons water

1 Bring the 3 cups water to a boil in a medium saucepan over medium heat. Add the knotted pandan leaves, if using. Add the tapioca and cook, stirring constantly, for 7 to 10 minutes, until the pearls have turned nearly translucent with some white spots in the middle.

2 Add the sugar and stir until it is completely dissolved. Add the cooked taro or corn, if using, and the young coconut with juice. Stir to combine. Remove from the heat and discard the pandan leaves, if using.

3 In another small saucepan, heat the coconut milk with the salt and stir until dissolved. Add the tapioca starch or cornstarch mixture. Stir well to combine and remove from heat.

4 Scoop the pudding into serving bowls and spoon 2 tablespoons of the coconut milk mixture over each portion. Serve chilled or at room temperature.

Sweet Sticky Rice and Mangoes

Khao Nieu Mamuang

Mango season in Thailand runs from March to May. The preferred variety for this dish is one called *mamuang ok rong*, which is very delicate and sweet. In North American markets, mango season generally runs from late April until mid-August or September; mangoes available year-round are the red-and-green Mexican variety known as Tommy Atkins, which tend to be stringy and not very sweet. But during the summer months, most Asian and some Western markets now offer mango varieties like Keitt, Ataulfo, Kent, Frances, and Haden. Any of these would be fine for capturing the essence of this classic Thai dessert. Thais usually steam the sticky rice in a woven cone-shaped bamboo basket that fits into a tall metal steamer. If you are using the more common type of steamer, be sure to line it with the cheesecloth to prevent the rice from slipping through the holes.

Preparation Time: 15 MINUTES, PLUS 6 HOURS FOR SOAKING
Cooking Time: 30 MINUTES
Makes 12 SERVINGS

3 cups (620 g) uncooked sticky rice
4 cups (1 liter) water
1½ cups (375 ml) coconut milk
1¼ cups (225 g) granulated sugar
1 teaspoon salt
6 ripe mangoes

1 Soak the rice in the water for 6 hours. Drain well. Line a steamer with cheesecloth, add the rice, and steam over boiling water for 20 to 30 minutes, or until the rice grains are tender.

2 Meanwhile, heat the coconut milk, sugar, and salt in a saucepan over medium-low heat, stirring, until dissolved. Remove ½ cup of the mixture and reserve for serving. Stir the cooked rice into the remaining coconut milk, mixing well. Cover, remove from heat, and let stand for 15 minutes; do not open the lid.

3 Slice the mangoes off their pits lengthwise so that there are 2 halves for each.

Cut each half crosswise into bite-sized pieces, but without cutting through the skin. Scoop out the pieces. To serve, spoon portions of sticky rice onto individual plates. Pour a little coconut milk mixture over top, and arrange mango slices around the rice.

Deep-Fried Bananas in Spring Roll Wrappers *Kluai Hom Pha*

There are more than 30 varieties of banana in Thailand, and Thais have created numerous recipes for this nutritious, often fragrant and usually inexpensive fruit. Green bananas are used in curries, while ripe bananas are made into desserts. For this recipe, the bananas should be ripe but still firm; otherwise they will fall apart in the wrappers and absorb too much oil. This dessert is delicious with vanilla ice cream.

Preparation Time: 5 MINUTES
Cooking Time: 10 MINUTES
Makes 12 PIECES

4 tablespoons brown sugar
¼ teaspoon ground cinnamon
Twelve 8-in (20-cm) round spring roll wrappers
6 ripe bananas, peeled, ends removed and sliced in half lengthwise
1 egg white, slightly beaten
3 cups (750 ml) vegetable oil for deep-frying
Honey or chocolate sauce for drizzling, as desired
Confectioners' sugar for sprinkling (optional)

1 Mix the brown sugar and cinnamon together. Set aside.

2 Place 1 spring roll wrapper on a flat surface. Set 1 banana piece, cut side up, on the wrapper near the edge closest to you. Sprinkle 1 teaspoon of the sugar-cinnamon mixture over the banana. Roll the banana up in the spring roll wrapper one or two times; fold the wrapper ends over the center to enclose the banana and continue to roll the banana up until completed. Seal with beaten egg white.

3 Heat the oil in a large wok to 350°F (175°C). Gently place a wrapped banana in the oil and cook until golden brown, about 3 minutes. Carefully remove with a slotted spoon and drain on paper towels. Repeat with the remaining bananas.

4 To serve, drizzle each piece with honey or chocolate sauce and sprinkle with confectioners' sugar, if desired.

Sweet Custard and Pumpkin

Sangkaya Fak Thong

This is not only a wonderful way to eat custard, but it makes a beautiful and unique presentation as well. Young green coconuts may be used instead of kabocha. You will need a large pot and steamer basket to make this dessert.

Pandan leaves, which come from a native Asian plant also known as screwpine, are available fresh or frozen from Asian markets. Pandan juice is simply the extract of the pandan leaf. Often referred to as "Asian vanilla," it adds a unique flavor to many Thai dishes. You can purchase the extract online or make your own; see page 20. Kabocha squash, also known as Japanese pumpkin, has an intense sweet flavor and a beautifully dense texture that is showcased in many Thai desserts. It is popular throughout many Asian countries, and is readily available at any Asian market.

Preparation time: 10 MINUTES
Cooking time: 60 TO 75 MINUTES
Makes 8 SERVINGS

1 small kabocha squash (Japanese
   pumpkin), about 2 lbs (900 g)
3 large eggs
1/3 cup (60 g) palm sugar
1/3 cup (60 g) granulated sugar
2/3 cup (160 ml) coconut milk
2 tablespoons Pandan Juice (page
   20)
1 tablespoon tapioca starch or
   cornstarch
1/2 teaspoon salt

1 Cut an opening at the top of the kabocha in a circle, square, or star shape. Discard the excised top. Scoop out and discard the seeds. Rinse the kabocha thoroughly, inside and out, and turn it upside down to dry.

2 In a mixing bowl, whisk together the eggs, palm sugar, and granulated sugar by hand until both sugars are dissolved. Add the coconut milk, pandan juice, and tapioca starch, and mix until all ingredients are well blended. Strain through a sieve to remove any lumps. Pour the egg mixture into the hollowed-out kabocha.

3 Cover the bottom of a large pot with water. Set the kabocha on a steamer rack above the water, cover, and bring to a boil over medium heat. Steam until the custard has set, 45 to 60 minutes. Check for doneness by inserting a toothpick in the center of the custard; if the toothpick comes out clean, it is done steaming. Carefully remove the kabocha from the steamer and refrigerate until well chilled. To make the custard firmer for easy slicing, briefly place the kabocha in the freezer.

4 Cut into 8 wedges, much as you would cut a round cake, and serve.

Thai Iced Coffee or Iced Tea

Kafee Yen

Long ago, Thais used to roast coffee beans with tamarind seeds. Nowadays, traditional Thai coffee may be made with roasted sesame seeds and corn as well. The Thai coffee used in this recipe should be available in Asian groceries. Look for a label that says *Oliang* powder, or Thai instant coffee, or both. *Oliang*, which comes from the Chaozhou dialect of Chinese, literally means "black" and "cold." So if you order *Oliang* in Thailand, you'll get a version of this drink without milk. When I was growing up, we used sweetened condensed milk in this drink. Serve with long-handled iced-tea spoons so your guests can stir the contrasting white milk and dark coffee together into a creamy blend. To make Thai Iced Tea, simply use the same amount of Thai tea powder, which is also available in Asian supermarkets, in place of the Thai instant coffee.

Cooking Time: 15 MINUTES
Makes 6 SERVINGS

6 cups (1.5 liters) water
$2/3$ cup (60 g) Thai coffee granules or powder
$1^{1}/_{4}$ cups (225 g) granulated sugar
1 cup (250 ml) evaporated milk or half-and-half

1 Bring the water to a rolling boil in a large saucepan. Add coffee powder, stirring just long enough to blend. Remove the pan from heat and let mixture steep for 10 minutes.

2 Pour the brew through a coffee filter or a fine-mesh strainer into a large coffee carafe or pitcher. Add the sugar to the hot coffee and stir to dissolve. Let cool to room temperature, cover and refrigerate until read to use.

3 At serving time, fill tall glasses with crushed ice. Add enough coffee to fill glass three-quarters full, then pour 3 tablespoons evaporated milk over the ice.

Thai Limeade

Nam Manao

Because Thailand is hot and humid all year round, Thais have developed many wonderful fresh-fruit drinks. Thai iced tea and iced coffee are also very popular. All these drinks are quite sweet, so you can have them as desserts, and not just as beverages.

Preparation Time: 5 MINUTES
Cooking Time: 10 MINUTES
Makes 6 TO 8 SERVINGS

7½ cups (1.75 liters) water
1½ cups (275 g) granulated sugar
1 cup (250 ml) fresh lime juice
1 teaspoon salt (optional)
Crushed ice

1 Combine 1½ cups (375 ml) water with the sugar in a saucepan and bring to a boil over medium heat. Reduce the heat to medium-low and cook for 7 to 10 minutes, or until the mixture becomes slightly syrupy. Let cool.

2 Add the lime juice, the remaining 6 cups water, and salt, if using, to the cooled syrup and stir well. To serve, fill tall glasses with crushed ice, pour the limeade over it, and add a straw.

Sources for Thai Ingredients

Most big cities have a market stocked with basic ingredients for cooking appealing Thai meals. If you can't find certain ingredients or equipment, you can order them online. Browse the internet or check out the following:

Thai supermarket online
importfood.com

Thai groceries
grocerythai.com

Thai grocery and kitchenware store
templeofthai.com

Asian supermarket
asiansupermarket365.com

Thai Asian grocery market
tastepadthai.com

Ethnic food shopping
ethnicfoodsco.com/Thailand/
ThaiHome.htm

Thailand groceries
onlinefoodgrocery.com/country/
thailand.html

Indian foods
store.indianfoodsco.com/
foods-of-thailgrocery-gc-th-0

Asian foods
veryasia.com

Thai supermarket
thaigrocer.com

Acknowledgments

To Alexandra Greeley who turned an idea into a reality. To Jeff Rosendhal, for photography. To Bob Diforio for finding a publisher. To Jon Keeton for editing and Tuttle for patience.

It's been an exciting journey from a village in Thailand to Bangkok, as a student, where I met Larry, a Peace Corps volunteer. To our children, Jenny and Mitch, whose love of Thai food make me so happy. To the patrons of the Thai Basil restaurant and my students, your support makes me work harder.

Along the way, there have been many others who helped and inspired me: my mother, a skilled home-cook; my sister Nit; Larry's family; the late Caroline Wagner, a personal hero, and Mel Wagner, my professor; Anne Blattberg, who said, "follow your dream," and Roger Blattberg, always supportive; Tina Nojek my first star student, and Gene Nojek, organizer of great food gatherings; my boss at the embassy in Beijing, Dr. Tom Yun, who upon tasting my food said, "Nong you are in the wrong business…open a restaurant"; to Wang Pei for help with my first cookbook; to Charas, a classmate, and Wai; to Peace Corps Thailand, Group III, Thailand, among my biggest boosters; to Nick and Ayhan, with whom we share a love of "T" countries; to our favorite landlord, Viroon, and our AUA and USIS Thai colleagues Thanit, Samlee and Wichai; to C.S. Yang and family who look after us in Bangkok; to friends from the USAID mafia; and to the members of Les Dames d'Escoffier, Washington DC, who encourage, support and offer sound advice; and of course to my hardworking staff.

To Bobby Flay, for giving Thai Basil a boost and Stephanie Feder, who helped me navigate Throwdown and a show featuring Samantha Brown, a wonderful, down-to-earth person. To fellow cookbook author, Nancie McDermott, who has given guidance and driven hundreds of miles to sample dishes. To David Thompson, for promoting Thai food culture, thanks for hosting me at Nahm in Bangkok. Finally, to my five grandchildren, I'll continue to share what I've learned in the kitchen with each of you.

Index

Published by Tuttle Publishing, an imprint of Periplus Editions (HK) Ltd.

www.tuttlepublishing.com

Copyright © 2015 Nongkran Daks and Alexandra Greeley

Library of Congress Cataloging-in-Publication Data

Nongkran Daks.
  Nong's Thai kitchen : 84 classic recipes that are quick, healthy and delicious / Nongkran Daks and Alexandra Greeley.
       pages cm
  Includes index.
  ISBN 978-0-8048-4331-7 (pbk.) -- ISBN 978-1-4629-1525-5 (ebook) 1. Cooking, Thai. I. Greeley, Alexandra. II. Title.
  TX724.5.T5N66 2015
  641.59593--dc23
                              2014030057

ISBN: 978-0-8048-4331-7

Distributed by
North America, Latin America & Europe
Tuttle Publishing
364 Innovation Drive
North Clarendon, VT 05759-9436 U.S.A.
Tel: (802) 773-8930; Fax: (802) 773-6993
info@tuttlepublishing.com
www.tuttlepublishing.com

Japan
Tuttle Publishing
Yaekari Building, 3rd Floor
5-4-12 Osaki, Shinagawa-ku
Tokyo 141 0032
Tel: (81) 3 5437-0171; Fax: (81) 3 5437-0755
sales@tuttle.co.jp
www.tuttle.co.jp

Asia Pacific
Berkeley Books Pte. Ltd.
61 Tai Seng Avenue #02-12
Singapore 534167
Tel: (65) 6280-1330; Fax: (65) 6280-6290
inquiries@periplus.com.sg
www.periplus.com

19 18 17 16 15   5 4 3 2 1
Printed in Malaysia   1503TW

TUTTLE PUBLISHING® is a registered trademark of Tuttle Publishing, a division of Periplus Editions (HK) Ltd.

The Tuttle Story: "Books to Span the East and West"

Many people are surprised to learn that the world's leading publisher of books on Asia had humble beginnings in the tiny American state of Vermont. The company's founder, Charles E. Tuttle, belonged to a New England family steeped in publishing.

Immediately after WWII, Tuttle served in Tokyo under General Douglas MacArthur and was tasked with reviving the Japanese publishing industry. He later founded the Charles E. Tuttle Publishing Company, which thrives today as one of the world's leading independent publishers.

Though a westerner, Tuttle was hugely instrumental in bringing a knowledge of Japan and Asia to a world hungry for information about the East. By the time of his death in 1993, Tuttle had published over 6,000 books on Asian culture, history and art—a legacy honored by the Japanese emperor with the "Order of the Sacred Treasure," the highest tribute Japan can bestow upon a non-Japanese.

With a backlist of 1,500 titles, Tuttle Publishing is more active today than at any time in its past—inspired by Charles Tuttle's core mission to publish fine books to span the East and West and provide a greater understanding of each.

Photo Credits